D0441332

"Anybody can be a bitch. And effe⟨ ⟩ run, in the long run (and it *is* a l⟨ ⟩ takes a woman who's smart, strong, and confident to assume the best from people and motivate them to deliver it. Daylle Deanna Schwartz shows you how to finish first—every time."

—GAIL BLANKE, author of *Throw Out Fifty Things: Clear the Clutter, Find Your Life*, life coach, and motivator

"Daylle Deanna Schwartz provides many constructive techniques for being soft-spoken, friendly, and considerate to others in ways that get satisfying results. This book is for women who are fundamentally nice, want to stay true to that, and who also want to be taken seriously, earn respect, and get their needs met."

—TERRIE M. WILLIAMS, author of *The Personal Touch: What You Really Need to Succeed in Today's Fast Paced Business World*

WITHDRAWN FROM CIRCULATION

"First as a therapist and later as an executive coach, I've worked with a lot of 'nice girls.' Most were trying to find ways to succeed while staying true to themselves. I would have loved to give each and every one of them a copy of this book!"

—CAROL KINSEY GOMAN, PH.D., author of *The Nonverbal Advantage: Secrets and Science of Body Language at Work*

"Women who live their lives as doormats fear that they will be viewed as a bitch if they learn how to say no and set boundaries with others. So they keep their heads low and allow others to trample all over them. But with this book these women can finally learn how to effectively take charge of their lives and finish on top while keeping their dignity intact. Thanks, Daylle, for an awesome and inspiring read!"

—DEBRA MANDEL, PH.D., psychologist and author of several books, including *Don't Call Me a Drama Queen!*

"Daylle Deanna Schwartz's newest book, *Nice Girls* Can *Finish First*, rocks! There are many women in my counseling practice who can use and benefit from the great exercises and information here. I really like Daylle's explanation of how to be a nice girl yet not become a people pleaser or a doormat. She outlines the pitfalls of being nice to others without being nice to yourself, and she shows girls how to say no, nicely. *Nice Girls* Can *Finish First* offers a really helpful self-empowerment tool kit, and the 'notes to self' are keepers. A very useful, practical, and helpful book for any young woman who wants to be nice, yet not walked over."

—TINA B. TESSINA, PH.D., psychotherapist and author of
many books, including *Money, Sex and Kids:
Stop Fighting About the Three Things
That Can Ruin Your Marriage*

NICE GIRLS
CAN FINISH FIRST

Getting the results you want and the respect you deserve
...While still being liked

DAYLLE DEANNA SCHWARTZ

New York   Chicago   San Francisco   Lisbon   London   Madrid   Mexico City
Milan   New Delhi   San Juan   Seoul   Singapore   Sydney   Toronto

The *McGraw·Hill* Companies

Library of Congress Cataloging-in-Publication Data

Schwartz, Daylle Deanna.
  Nice girls can finish first : getting the results you want and the respect you
deserve—while still being liked / Daylle Deanna Schwartz.
      p.   cm.
  Includes bibliographical references and index.
  ISBN 978-0-07-160907-4 (alk. paper)
  1. Women—Life skills guides.   I. Title.

HQ1221.S35   2009
646.70082—dc22   2008040558

*This book is dedicated to the memory of my beloved parents,
Lt. Colonel Robert C. Herman and Ruth Herman, for their
consistent, deep, unconditional love and support. They
instilled values in me that made me want to be nice to
people, despite the saying that nice guys finish last.*

Copyright © 2009 by Daylle Deanna Schwartz. All rights reserved. Printed in the United
States of America. Except as permitted under the United States Copyright Act of 1976, no
part of this publication may be reproduced or distributed in any form or by any means,
or stored in a database or retrieval system, without the prior written permission of the
publisher.

1 2 3 4 5 6 7 8 9 10 11 12 13 14 15 16 17 18 19 20 21   FGR/FGR   0 9 8

ISBN 978-0-07-160907-4
MHID   0-07-160907-5

Interior design by Monica Baziuk

McGraw-Hill books are available at special quantity discounts to use as premiums and
sales promotions or for use in corporate training programs. To contact a representative,
please visit the Contact Us pages at www.mhprofessional.com.

This book is printed on acid-free paper.

Contents

Acknowledgments

As always, I must begin by thanking God for all of my blessings. Without my strong belief in Him, I wouldn't be where I am today! Faith allows and encourages me to continue to treat people nicely and take care of myself as well.

Thank you to my dedicated agent, Linda Konner, for your strong belief in me and my writing, for your ongoing support, and for all your hard work on my behalf. Thank you to my fabulous editor at McGraw-Hill, Johanna Bowman, for your enthusiasm about my writing and for being a pleasure to work with; and thanks to Emily Carlton, my current editor, for also being a pleasure to work with.

Big, big thanks to my teeny, wonderfully supportive family—Tami and Lonny Kramer, Carla Herman, Doug Landy, Charlie and Carol Snyder. And thanks to my friends who supported me through my growing pains as I evolved from being a DoorMat into a nice girl who gets what she needs by being a Nice Girl on Top! Thank you Ellen Penchansky, my best friend in the universe, for always cheering me on as I found my way. Thank you Julie Coulter for your always-cheerful love and encouragement. Thank you Nasrin Sahihi, for being such a good friend by e-mail from Tehran.

A special thanks to everyone at the Moonstruck diner on Second Avenue and 58th Street in New York City, where I regularly take my laptop out for a yummy meal, several coffee refills, and terrific service from my special waitress, Hedia.

Introduction

"First they ignore you, then they laugh at you,
then they fight you, then you win."

—MAHATMA GANDHI

I'M A RECOVERING DoorMat. For years I let people walk all over me, taking advantage of my people-pleasing nature. I learned early that if I made others more important than me, they liked me. And I needed to be liked! Since I wasn't thin, I did favors to compensate. Eventually the pain of feeling used, taken for granted, and having my needs ignored pushed me to develop self-respect. It took years to become the confident, happy, nice girl I am today—what I call a Nice Girl on Top. Now people look elsewhere to wipe their feet, and it feels great! I'm still a nice person, and *my* needs get met too. You can be soft-spoken *and* kind *and* get taken seriously. You can say no and still be liked. I'll show you how!

When I appeared on "Oprah," she asked the audience whether they preferred being liked or respected. Everyone chose liked. Woman after woman described how much she did for others and affirmed that being liked was way more important than being inconvenienced by others—by spending money on gifts, lending money, performing chores, and more! I wasn't surprised, because I used to act the same way in order to have some company, and it really hurt to be let down repeatedly by someone I was good to. Many women are raised to be People Pleasers. Good little girls please for acceptance and grow into acquiescent women who continue the pattern.

Do you hate being taken advantage of? It hurts when no one supports you, especially if you please everyone. Does feeling unappreciated lower your self-esteem? Do you want to be kind, friendly, and soft-spoken and still get your way? It's time to feel good about your desire to be nice. Nice Girls on Top are caring, kind people who take care of themselves in soft-spoken ways that achieve results. You can gain satisfaction by redefining *nice*. The healthy kind of nice rocks!

✿ Living as a DoorMat ✿

Being a People Pleaser hurts confidence and self-image if you don't know how to set boundaries defining how much to give and how to get your needs satisfied too. I grew up believing people would like me more if I were agreeable. Small girls seemed to get more. I thought pleasing everyone would take attention away from my larger body. I stayed on agreeable autopilot until I recognized some self-worth and began a transition that I call my *journey into self.* Today people know me as a confident, self-sufficient woman. Yet my self-esteem was in the toilet for many years. I suffered from DoorMat syndrome on many levels after I left my utopian world of caring family and neighbors to live in the "real" world.

I grew up in a cocoon of "nice" in the Bronx—a loving family and kind neighbors. Mom was very giving, so it was natural to follow her pattern. But her kindness was reciprocated. As I grew older, new friends took advantage of my giving nature. My self-image was skewed by perceptions in the media. All I saw in the mirror was cellulite, and I felt fat and ugly. To compensate, I sacrificed my needs to be liked. People took without consideration. I felt used, unappreciated, and confused, with no survival skills for handling one-way takers. My home environment left me unprepared.

In adulthood, I got lost. Life had no passion or challenge as I followed directives. My aunt drummed into me that teaching was the only career for women. I grew up responding to what I wanted to be with "anything but a teacher." But what's a "good girl" to do when her college adviser says otherwise? I had high math SAT scores and wanted to study a creative business field, but my adviser pushed me into liberal arts, saying I didn't need a career since I'd get a husband to take care of me! My dreams were squashed.

After I graduated at twenty, my college sweetheart and I were pushed to marry by our parents. We'd been together for three years—my entire adult life! It felt too soon. I'd never been on my own and wanted to develop as a woman first. But I did as I was told and went directly from being someone's daughter to being someone's wife. With few options, I followed my husband into teaching and felt my soul die. Before my wedding, my heart said to fly. Friends said it was prewedding jitters. I knew better but deluded myself. I was too insecure to take off.

My husband was a good man who enjoyed my giving. Friends did too. I gave rides, had kids dumped on me, helped with anything, and felt trapped. For years I believed it was all my fault. Plus, I needed to feel needed. Doing favors was insurance against being alone. I truly felt like a DoorMat—flat and useless. I fantasized about using my creativity in satisfying ways. But insecurity and fear of stepping outside my safety zone blocked my taking a risk.

My dream was to be a whole person, not just what others expected! Going through the motions of my roles became habit. I felt comatose, passing time instead of living as passions went unfulfilled. My personal identity was lost by living for everyone but me. Who was Daylle as an individual? In the mirror I saw a scared woman with cellulite and unruly hair. How could I leave if I felt too worthless to attract a man? I still believed I needed one to complete me. Until, that is, I began working on my self-esteem.

Several "Aha!" moments in a row woke me a little about my value as a person. They motivated me to practice giving my needs more priority and showing myself love as I began to appreciate me. Slowly I became more selective about doing favors for friends, which felt wonderful, but they didn't like it. As I silently exalted in my newfound freedom from being the go-to girl, I was accused of turning into a bitch! It was confusing since all I did was turn down favors when it was inconvenient. *Bitch* hit me like a knife, and I ran back to my DoorMat ways. It felt yucky to be disliked. I struggled to stand up for myself without losing friends.

My turning point was a night my husband and I had planned to eat Italian food. I'd never said no to him, but I didn't feel well and wanted a different restaurant. He was used to acquiescence and insisted on Italian: "Join me or not." "Not!" I said. He was stunned, but he left alone. I felt empowered. Later he warned I was turning into a bitch. Excuse me? I was a bitch because I couldn't eat Italian food with indigestion? No more letting poison words stop my progress! I began to believe I deserved happiness. Why always go along with others when few reciprocated?

My needs were important too. I wasn't a bitch. As the sting of it passed, I accepted I was still a nice person—on my way out of Door-Matville! If that meant being called a bitch, so be it. I had done nothing wrong. This revelation fueled me to take control of my life and develop a personal identity beyond other people's expectations.

✈ The Train out of DoorMatville ✈

Like many People Pleasers, I'd been proud to be nice until I accepted that being a DoorMat wasn't nice. Now I was pissed. How could he use me when I'd been so kind? How could she take such a good friend for granted? And the hardest—after helping many people—why did I have no one to count on? I declared independence from DoorMatville and tried the bitch route. People took me more seriously but didn't like me. Worse—I didn't like me.

I did a U-turn to a more empowered kind of nice, with a healthier balance between taking care of me and helping others. Slowly respect came with taking myself seriously. I learned to get my way without raising my voice and embraced being nice. My new demeanor showed it was possible to be what I call a Nice Girl on Top. I began a journey that proves a DoorMat can take charge of her world. I'm blessed to have been able to reinvent myself, many times, despite warnings that it was too late for me since I had no experience or education to follow my passions. *Not! Can'ts* and *shoulds* became obsolete.

My quest for creative outlets led me to become the first white female rapper and one of the first women to start an independent record label. While I was teaching school, students said I couldn't make a rap record because I was a white woman. Hello! I had to teach them not to let stereotypes stop them, so I learned to rap and recorded "Girls Can Do." The kids loved it and encouraged me to shop my music. I hired people who ripped me off. Students offered to get revenge by slashing tires and performing other nasty deeds. That's not nice! I opened Revenge Productions, then Revenge Records, to teach them to use the energy behind anger for something positive.

My first record generated media attention. Nicknamed "the rappin' teach," I learned by making painful and costly mistakes. Attending music conferences the first year felt bad. People saw my name badge and acted like I wasn't worth speaking to. A majority of women dressed very provocatively, showing a willingness to open doors with sex. That made it harder for women who took themselves seriously. Sex was expected in return for favors. My appearance didn't invite sex. Yet the attitude was pervasive.

I met a very powerful music industry player in his sixties (I'll call him Lou) who said he believed in me and even assured my parents he'd protect me. After giving guidance and encouragement, he caught me completely off guard when he suddenly and forcefully groped me inappropriately. As I protested, he warned that I needed to learn to play the game and I'd never succeed if I didn't give up sex.

My Nice Girl on Top kicked in, and I warned him back: let go or I'd hurt him and call the police. Whenever I doubted whether I could have a successful record label without "playing the game," that memory motivated me. After releasing two rap records that sold well, I wrote a song called "Never Again," signed an artist, and worked hard to market it. It put my label, and me as a songwriter, on the music industry map. I then wrote a dance track called "Sensual Power" and sang it. It did well both in the United States and overseas! I continued writing songs and signing artists and went from being ignored at conferences to speaking on panels. Not bad for a recovering DoorMat! When I saw Lou at a conference, he expressed respect for me, wished me well, and offered his help. I politely declined.

I needed confidence to dance with the boys in the industry as one of the few women with a record label. I read everything I could find on music business, went to conferences, and consulted with experts. After educating myself thoroughly, I experienced more success, which made me very confident and determined to earn respect.

I tested my Nice Girls on Top techniques. Knowing that acting tough would alienate me, I put on a smile, let comments roll off, and worked very hard. I learned to speak in ways that got noticed. It took time, but by consistently being friendly and courteous with a firm and serious demeanor, I became a member of the boys' club. No one dared make a pass or try to take advantage. But they liked me, and it was fun!

✒ Living at the Top ✒

. . . .

As music stimulated my soul, I traded my lifestyle coma for happiness. My self-confidence grew, and I felt more complete. It put more stress on my marriage. My husband and I amicably decided to separate. Part of me was terrified. But a bigger part was exhilarated about finally embarking on a life with choices. What a joy it was to live for me for the first time! To this day, I enjoy satisfying simple needs such as eating when *I'm* hungry, sleeping when *I'm* tired, and just putting me first. But friends couldn't relate to my wanting autonomy and disappeared. Perhaps it hit too close to their own unhappy situations.

I ran Revenge Records for five years and still taught school, which I didn't want to do any longer. I don't know how much further I'd have gotten had a friend not insisted I read a book that opened the door to my biggest blessing—faith! I considered myself an atheist. The book made me realize I already lived a somewhat spiritual lifestyle and motivated me to embrace very strong faith in the universe and then God. I knew serious risks were needed to pursue my passions. As faith got stronger, it gave me the courage to blow off my income sources, close my label, leave my inexpensive house share, and move into a wonderful apartment in midtown Manhattan without knowing how I'd support myself.

The first year I did substitute teaching. While it was easy and convenient, it felt like selling out. I did not want to spend my time teaching. With God's support, I vowed never to do another thing I wasn't passionate about, and once I quit teaching after that first year, I never looked back nor did work I didn't love again.

I found a variety of fun freelance gigs and began leading workshops on my areas of expertise. People kept asking how to start a record label. So I taught music biz classes at an adult ed program at first. Then I took charge, rented a hotel room, and marketed private workshops myself. When asked for how-tos on becoming self-empowered while still being nice, I began my Nice Girls on Top workshops and self-empowerment counseling. I always had an M.S. to be a therapist, but how could a DoorMat help others? Now I could!

Today I'm a successful author, speaker, blogger ("Lessons from a Recovering DoorMat"), self-empowerment counselor, and music industry consultant—a far cry from DoorMatville! I even rereleased my rap track, "Girls Can Do," and "Sensual Power," my dance track, on iTunes. Now I want to help you create your own journey to becoming a woman who gets her needs met, is taken seriously, feels confident, embraces happiness, gains the respect of everyone in the room when she enters it, and is still soft-spoken and kind—a Nice Girl on Top!

An Empowered Kind of Nice

There's a big difference between being nice and being a Door-Mat. Don't lose your pleasure in helping people. Nice Girls on Top choose whom to go the distance for and protect themselves from being taken advantage of. *Nice Girls* Can *Finish First* focuses on effective methods to get needs met. It's not traditional assertiveness, and it offers a practical alternative attitude and effective techniques for handling situations and people in courteous ways that ensure results.

In your search for acceptance, you can lose yourself. Chasing perfection reinforces how imperfect you are. I finally recognized we all make mistakes and have imperfections. But the media emphasizes perfection, making it difficult to appreciate yourself as you are. Do not allow people pleasing to compensate for your shortcomings. Even beautiful, successful women feel inadequate because they believe they're not good enough, mirroring the media and unhealthy behaviors they see around them. They point out the pound they need to lose or a facial line only they can see. You might hate those beautiful, complaining women who seem to have it so good. But they were raised like the rest of us and don't see it. They, too, feel insecure.

The ability for women to empower themselves has changed dramatically since the first feminists stood up and encouraged women to be more assertive and fight for the education, career, job, or work hours they needed. During the feminist revolution, the great Bella Abzug said, "Women have been trained to speak softly and carry a lipstick. Those days are over." Nice Girls on Top find a comfortable middle ground—between a traditional "good girl" who can't set boundaries and a woman who feels she can't be soft and sweet and be taken seriously. You can speak softly, be attractive and feminine, wear lipstick, *and* be empowered. This book provides tools to transition from a People Pleaser to a woman who takes control of her life, respectfully, nicely.

Nice Girls Can *Finish First* begins by explaining the difference between a nice girl who finishes last (DoorMat) and one who finishes first (Nice Girl on Top). Then I discuss factors that bust your power and begin introducing constructive tools you can use immediately—baby steps—to break old habits with techniques that will confuse people. You'll still be a soft, kind woman yet make a big impact with how you speak and carry yourself. Folks will have to take you seriously! From there I provide suggestions for getting stronger on the inside.

I left techniques for turning people down for later in the book, so you can build confidence first. There are also constructive ways to set boundaries and communicate effectively, with specific tips for handling uncomfortable situations with parents, friends, roommates, service people, romantic partners, and others in softer, more comfortable ways that still mean business. The book concludes with strategies for getting more respect at work and advice for advancing and staying on top.

Are you afraid you'll alienate people by standing up for yourself or asking for what you want? You *can* take control of your life and still be liked! Allow me to help you grow into a Nice Girl on Top. Leo Durocher said, "Nice guys finish last." That's garbage! When you understand the true definition of *nice,* you can practice being considerate and respectful to everyone while employing techniques in this book to be nice and still finish *first.* I'm kind, considerate, and give as much to people in need as I possibly can— and I still get what I want.

In the following pages I'll share lessons and techniques learned in my journey from a people-pleasing DoorMat to a Nice Girl on Top. This book provides new ways to stop unacceptable behavior, get needs met, ask for more, agree to do fewer undesired favors, and be well liked, without resorting to pleasing everyone beyond normal courtesy. I wish you positive growth and a delightful, fulfilling rise to the top!

1

Nice Girls Who Finish Last

"I know that we will be the sufferers if we let great wrongs occur without exerting ourselves to correct them."

—ELEANOR ROOSEVELT

NICE HAS BECOME almost generic. Things, people, places, or situations can be nice—even weather. *Nice* is considered a nice word. So if *nice* is so nice, why do many believe a nice girl gets much less and isn't as attractive to men? This chapter gives a brief overview of factors that reinforce the need to please and how that can lead to being the kind of nice girl who does finish last. Awareness of where behavior comes from begins self-empowerment.

✈ People Pleaser Mentality ✈

"The reasonable man adapts himself to the world: the unreasonable one persists in trying to adapt the world to himself."

—GEORGE BERNARD SHAW

DMS (DOORMAT SYNDROME) made me a People Pleaser who catered to others, with little reciprocation. People Pleasers don't turn down requests or assert their needs. Do you want to stop one-way favors but don't know how? It hurts to give and give and feel used. Been there, done that! I want you to understand the syndrome so you can watch for signs and break old habits. Once you understand why you've been a People Pleaser, you can use my tools to get your needs met nicely by slowly transitioning into a Nice Girl on Top. If I can do it, anyone can! Here are some common reasons for pleasing.

Buying into Sexual Stereotypes

Like me, many girls receive more emphasis on marriage and kids than on developing a life/career and aren't taught to value their abilities. Heidi says, "No one ever told me I did a good job." Girls are often treated as more fragile, which decreases self-confidence. Boys are seen as more competent. Needing a man to feel complete implies you're not whole. Stereotypes imply that pleasing everyone and keeping your mouth shut is best. It takes soul-searching and consciousness to accept that you're entitled to be happy on your own. Letitia is fighting old messages:

> I always pleased everyone, except me of course. Growing up, I got more attention for my appearance than my skills. I wanted to learn to fix things, but Dad only taught my brothers. They had more freedom. I was warned about getting hurt if I tried new things and felt incapable. In college I took a woodworking class and didn't saw off my arm as Dad feared. I became darn good but was pushed into teaching. I'm still longing to pursue carpentry, but after years of being told I'm not capable, it's hard to find the confidence.

"I Like Being Nice"

Some of us simply enjoy being nice because it feels good to be liked by other people. But those who enjoy helping people don't protect themselves from getting taken advantage of. Helping others and being needed both create a false sense of being wanted. Do you want to be liked for what you do or for who you are? In Chapter 2, I redefine *nice*. If you set boundaries, you can enjoy pleasing people in more satisfying ways.

An Unhappy Childhood

Being a People Pleaser in an unloving home can score points. Sometimes kids are physically or mentally abused and pleasing earns them better treatment. It can keep an abusive parent calm. A protective pattern of pleasing everyone can continue into adulthood. Habits can be broken!

A Happy Childhood

Strangely enough, a nurturing upbringing can set you up to be a DoorMat. Seeing people through the rose-colored glasses of childhood creates a naive attitude that keeps your guard down in the outside world. My loving parents, friends, and neighbors helped each other—it was a cocoon of love and caring. I gave a lot but received too. Leaving home was a shock! After an ideal world of nice, I was unprepared for people taking without giving back and had no tools to protect myself. It took years to adjust into a Nice Girl on Top.

Fear of Loneliness

Some People Pleasers go out of their way to please or pay tabs to avoid being alone. I thought food tasted better with company and treated whoever joined me for dinner! Discomfort with being alone often leads to buying friends with favors and other currency. But it hurts to wonder if they'd be there without perks. After attending my class, Lilly is less scared of loneliness than of feeling used. She learned her friends really weren't friends:

> *I liked having lots of friends and made sure to please everyone and play chauffeur, but I made all the overtures! People called only to confirm a favor. I wondered if anyone would notice if I disappeared, except for losing my services, and stopped calling. I was appalled that nobody called and knew I'd always been alone. That got me to this class.*

"I'm Not Worthy!"

Low self-esteem sets you up to get taken advantage of. But if you don't like yourself, why should others like you? Childhood criticism or a focus on your imperfections creates a tendency to put your needs aside to pursue approval. Emily says, "Inadequacy still makes me go overboard to please and unable to receive." You can discover your worthiness! I'll show you how.

Feeling Fat (aka Not Being Thin Enough)

Body image is a *huge* self-empowerment buster. Many girls believe that if they're not thin, they're fat. I was a tall child. It made me feel big, which translated into fat. Looking at photos, I can see that I was never fat. But I tried harder to please since my value felt less than that of the small, popular girls. Body perception gets distorted as a child and continues into adulthood, with comparisons to airbrushed women and self-hatred for not being perfect. You can fix the perceptions you get from the distorted mirror you see yourself in.

❧ Good Girls Who Don't Feel Good ❧

. . . .

*"I don't know the key to success, but the key to
failure is trying to please everybody."*
—BILL COSBY

FEAR AND INSECURITY trigger behavior that keeps gears stuck in People Pleaser mode. Are you really happy doing favors at your own expense? Nice Girls on Top accept their right to be happy. Read on and decide which you want to be. Watch for any mentality that may guide your behavior.

"Me Last"

Do you get conflicted between what people *expect* from you and what you *want*? People Pleasers get disappointed when people don't keep their word or support them. Self-pity flourishes: "Why me? I try so hard." But they don't know how to stop the cycle. It can seem easier to placate than take a stand, but the price—your happiness—is too high.

"Don't Pick on Me!"/"Please Notice Me"

People Pleasers say they kiss up for attention, to avoid getting picked on, or to feel included. The class bully goes elsewhere for potshots if he gets your lunch. Mom may not hit you if you jump to her wishes. Quiet kids get lost in a big family or in someone's shadow. Being useful gets noticed. Everyone likes some attention, but purposely being nice to those who aren't nice to you hurts. Sharon said in a class:

> *I've always been shy and more comfortable being nice to people than speaking. When I did homework for classmates, I had com-*

pany. Helping makes me feel wanted and noticed. I'm the go-to person at work for all problems. It's a big place, and I'd feel lost otherwise. I want to change but still need attention.

Chasing Acceptance

Most of us want to fit in. The need to please increases as you pursue acceptance. It's hard to be on top if you're always someone's welcome mat. When you accept yourself, you'll get acceptance for the right reasons. Bridgett says:

My parents divorced when I was young, and my father became distant. He noticed what I did wrong faster than what I did right. I craved approval so much I'd do almost anything for him. It transferred to anyone I cared about, especially men, who call me needy. I hate that! I'm trying to stop chasing approval but still feel so inadequate.

Kvetching Inside and Out

People Pleasers believe that expressing needs or, heaven forbid, anger isn't part of the equation for being liked. But anger won't miraculously dissolve. People Pleasers often complain and complain to friends who tolerate it, but not to the person causing your anger. This book will help you develop skills and confidence to stop complaining and stand up to bad behavior. Then you can kvetch about the weather!

All of the preceding behavior is common in many women. It's not something to beat yourself up over or see as a weakness. Let me help you finish first. Having been to the bottom, I know how sweet the top can be!

2

Nice Girls Who Finish First

========

"The willingness to accept responsibility for one's own
life is the source from which self-respect springs."

—JOAN DIDION

Nice girls can finish first. This recovering DoorMat attests
to that! As a Nice Girl on Top, I give more than ever. When
you're nice to yourself first, you have more for others, in healthier
ways. There's nothing nice about being unhappy, no matter how
many are happy as a result of your sacrifice. Focus on your own
bliss! I'll give you a map and tools to navigate.

❧ When *Nice* Isn't *Nice* ❧

"Only in growth, reform and change is true security to be found."
—ANNE MORROW LINDBERGH

Do you do favors to compensate for what you see as your shortcomings and call it being nice? Feeling out of control in situations
with colleagues, men, your mom, and others can make you more
accommodating to their needs than to your own. The price:

▶ You're not taken seriously.
▶ Your needs aren't met, and favors aren't reciprocated.
▶ You're taken for granted.
▶ You're afraid to express yourself.
▶ You're angry deep down, while making nice to folks.
▶ Your self-image is lower than it could be.

That's not nice!

Nice vs. DoorMat

Nice people complain they try hard to be nice, yet people don't reciprocate:

▶ "I was good to Rob, going along with whatever he wanted. I'd cook and buy him gifts. But he left me. Why do nice girls always get hurt?"
▶ "I rarely turn people down, but they rarely help me. Being nice sucks!"
▶ "I always give people what they want, but they walk over me. Why aren't nice people appreciated?"

This illustrates the wrong side of nice. Putting more energy into pleasing others than into making yourself happy, often at your own expense, isn't nice. It's being a DoorMat! That reality hurts, Robin says:

I prided myself on being nice. Growing up, I got attention only by helping people. So I've always gone out of my way to please, even those who didn't treat me well. I said yes to requests without thinking and deluded myself that everyone loved me. But deep down I doubted it since I got little back. My husband teased that I was the world's caretaker. I laughed, with tears underneath. It wasn't until my six-year-old noticed that I faced the truth—my desire to be liked devalued me. When I broke my leg, we took a cab to the store—everyone was busy. Jessica heard me ask for help and asked why nobody ever helped me. I didn't want to be a bad role model, so I thought before giving. It felt better than the price for being liked. Now being nice includes me!

NOTE TO SELF: There's a *huge* difference between being a healthy kind of nice and giving yourself away.

Nice does *not* mean doing favors indiscriminately or always being agreeable. Nice Girls on Top are kind to others and themselves too. People Pleasers don't set limits on how much to give—and call it nice. Hello! That's not nice! It's buying friends with favors. Girlfriends! Accept the truth—that kind of behavior isn't nice! Jenn says:

I was an obese child and knew how hurtful people can be, so I went to the extreme to be nice to everyone. I was always the first person to make new kids in school feel welcomed, and it felt good to make others feel good. But at a certain point it crosses the line to where you start sacrificing yourself, and it's something to be conscious of. Aside from lowered self-esteem and not feeling in control, I felt resentful toward situations and myself. I found it very draining to feel guilty all the time, and it created negative energy for my way of being.

Do you complain that people take advantage of how nice you are? Hmm. How sincerely nice are you? Fuming that you don't get back for what you give? Hurt when people don't support you after all you've done for them? When you pay a store cashier, you get a product. When you do favors and are willingly manipulated, you may get an empty shopping cart. Expecting reciprocation for

being nice isn't nice. Real nice doesn't expect support or friendship from doing favors. Michelle says:

> *Being too nice made me feel used, undervalued, and frustrated*
> *because I didn't really understand why I let it happen. Underneath*
> *the surface, I was angry at others who were oblivious to the fact*
> *that they were taking advantage of me and upsetting me, and I*
> *was angrier at myself for not being able to articulate my needs and*
> *feelings clearly.*

Are you afraid people will disappear if you stop being nice? I
was. Oh, I thought I was soooooo nice. Ms. Saint. But I was really
Ms. Wimp, Ms. Victim. I complained to everyone that people I
catered to didn't reciprocate my kindness. So, I wasn't really nice.
I was an oxymoron—calling myself nice, yet whining to anyone
who'd listen about how people weren't nice to me. I never considered that I should be nice to me. When I called myself a former
oxymoron, Liza said:

> *I don't know if I'm an oxymoron or just a moron. I've always lived*
> *to be nice. But I ask myself if it's nice to feel anger toward many*
> *people. I'm tired of not getting rewarded for being nice. They take*
> *and ignore me. But waiting to be rewarded isn't being nice. I never*
> *have time for what I want because I've committed to others. So*
> *maybe I'm just an unnice moron.*

EXERCISE: Divide a sheet of paper into two columns. Think back
over the last week and write down everything nice you did for
someone else on the left side and everything nice you did for
yourself on the right side. If the right side isn't longer than the
left, become conscious of doing more to change that.

Were you taught to be agreeable to keep the peace? How peaceful do you feel? Don't *you* count too? A woman's sense of self often depends on personal relationships, so they're maintained at all costs. But your needs shouldn't take a backseat to others! Keep *you* in the giving equation. If you do the People Pleaser dance, be careful. People get tired of it. Did you ever date a guy who went overboard to please? "I'll do anything you like." That's a turnoff! You almost smell desperation. Even DoorMats lose interest in other DoorMats. People Pleasers can make friends grab a life preserver—space. People don't want to risk hurting such a nice person or feel obligated to return excessive kindness. It hurt to wonder if anyone liked me for me. Emily identifies:

> *I was brought up to be agreeable and got praised for favors. Insecurity made me jump when asked for something so I'd be liked. When a friend asked why I was so insecure, I was shocked it was obvious. She pointed out my good qualities and that I didn't need to cater to be liked. Her praise for my attributes improved my self-image, and I slowly did more for me. Now I know which friends actually like me. Those who seem annoyed I don't jump anymore can disappear!*

 NOTE TO SELF: If you give lots, but people aren't nice back at ya, it hurts—not nice!

I wasn't happy on "agreeable autopilot" but acted like everything was fine as I helped someone who called only for favors. I lived in fantasy—deluding myself that I had good friends while I sort of knew the truth. I understand People Pleasers. Everyone wants to be liked. That's normal. But when you're troubled by behavior that fulfills that need, it's time to reevaluate it. Pleasing provides false security. Is that worth knowing you're being used and not getting your needs met? Robin decided it's not:

> *I didn't feel pretty. Cute girls got more, so I compensated by being the agreeable one. Everyone liked what I did for them, but I hoped they'd like me. I joined a women's group, and the leader asked what makes us happy. I was ashamed to say having friends who liked me! I found a therapist and slowly became happier solo than with friends I had bought with favors. My self-confidence grew as I stopped feeling beaten up by "friends" who used me. I found a new job and met people who didn't know me as a People Pleaser. I have fewer friends but they're real!*

If you want to be happier, be kind to you too! A Nice Girl on Top gives if she can, selectively. Redefine *nice*! You'll have more time for you, receive more positive responses, and earn respect too.

Spiritual vs. People Pleaser

Some women were brought up with strong religious/spiritual values and feel lost about how to handle feeling used. I have a strong spiritual core and believed that God wanted me to please everyone. Women often say they show God's love by helping others. But what about being good to you? Kind people need boundaries. When religion teaches you to help others, it's confusing if it hurts. A Nice Girl on Top helps others *and* herself. You can only do your best and are entitled to take care of you.

NOTE TO SELF: Spiritual doesn't mean being a DoorMat or sacrificing for everyone who wants something.

I try my best to treat others as I believe God wants me to but still keep me in the picture. You're entitled to protect yourself. Taking care of you first leaves more energy for others. Anger at people who don't return kindness isn't spiritual. Spiritual also isn't being a charity for everyone. LaTonya learned:

> *My minister preaches we should treat others as we want to be treated. That contradicted feeling like a loser after being taken advantage of. If God wants us to be good to others, why did being nice make me feel hurt and undervalued? I discussed it with my minister, who explained that a good person doesn't sacrifice for everyone. God wants us to do the best we can. Saying no and asking for more is spiritual. I'm one of God's children, and He wants me to receive and be happy.*

I know that God wants me included in being good to others. Don't stop helping people. Find a balance for giving and for getting your needs met too. Now I love to help when possible to be kind, not to score points or have it returned, but I'm also nice to me.

✒ Waking Up and Smelling ✒ the Cappuccino

. . . .

"If you are not ready today, you will be even less so tomorrow."

—Ovid

A NICE GIRL on Top is soft-spoken, friendly, and considerate, while getting what she needs. People take her seriously because she takes herself seriously. Ask yourself:

▶ Do I like making everyone more important than me?

▶ Does feeling needed make up for feeling lousy when taken for granted?

▶ Is having "friends" worth buying them with favors?

You know the answers. No one likes feeling like a DoorMat. You *can* make a conscious decision to be there for yourself first.

Taking "Welcome" off Your Mat

People in my classes believe being nice makes people take advantage. Yet they keep on giving and get hurt, angry, bitter. The stereotypical nice girl:

▶ Cuts everyone extra slack about unfair treatment—at the expense of self-worth

▶ Forgives everyone easily—except herself

▶ Can be counted on day or night—yet wonders why people aren't nice to her

These nice girls often do finish last. Not knowing the results of standing up to people can seem risky. Mary said in a class:

> *Co-workers arrive late, take long lunches, and waste time on personal e-mails. Their output suffers, so I'm pressed to work weekends to do their work and hate it. I work harder for the same money! My boss takes advantage. When I get backed up after helping someone slow, he won't get me help and says "Work faster." I rarely get thanks. To me nice means "sucker"! But I need my job and want to be liked, so I stew privately.*

I told Mary it was her choice to let him take advantage. So she told her boss she had weekend plans and continued making excuses until he stopped asking. Mary also slowed down since working fast wasn't appreciated and took breaks with colleagues. When her boss complained, she nicely explained she was working like everyone else. Her boss got the message and showed more appreciation. Mary learned people can't take you for granted without your consent. Naomi learned growing up:

> *I was raised not to care what other people thought of me so long as I respect what other people think of themselves because it is only then one can truly respect and value one's own identity and worth.*

You can learn now! Nice people are entitled to say no and to address behavior that feels wrong. If you don't purposely hurt someone, why not honor your needs? Do folks say it's selfish? Get over it! Why is taking care of you selfish? Consider it rationally, without guilt. Why create false security by making others happy if you aren't happy too? Verna says:

> *If I thought someone didn't like me, I'd do more favors. My cousin asked why I never worried about me, pointing out I'm always stressed about others. It was true. While I hoped for security, I was very insecure about never being good enough. She lectured that people like favors, not me, and I deserve much better. I listened. And pondered her words—a lot. Slowly I curtailed favors. It's painful to know someone doesn't like me, but now I accept it instead of trying to buy them.*

When I was a hard-core People Pleaser, several caring friends said I deserved much better. It opened my eyes a little, helped me notice my good qualities, and increased my self-appreciation. Jen says, "I have grown much stronger as a person by making myself and what I want a bigger priority. This makes me feel more in control of myself." She lived with a boyfriend who dismissed her thoughts. She always caved in during fights and felt no control over her life, trapped since she didn't earn enough to support herself:

It was scary—knowing I was with the wrong person, yet finan-cially powerless to leave. I did anything to avoid conflicts and wouldn't stand up for what I wanted. I was complacent and in some ways living in fear, afraid of where my life was going and how long I would live with him. Would he break up with me? I thought of all my dreams and knew my boyfriend didn't take them seri-ously. He wasn't supportive, had no confidence in me, and thought I would never accomplish what was important to me. Eventually I believed maybe I couldn't do them, they weren't as important as I thought, or they were stupid and childish. I tried to forget them, but they wouldn't go away. Every time we fought, I escaped to a place where I was happy with myself and working hard to achieve dreams that didn't seem out of reach. After an all-night argument that wasn't resolved, I woke up and finally admitted I was living a lie. I was unhappy. Life was too short to be miserable. I did not like the person I was living with and was angry he did not care about what was important to me and even angrier with myself. I did not like the person I had let myself become. I vowed never to let pride, stubbornness, and fear control me again.

 NOTE TO SELF: When your own opinion sets your standards, you're in charge.

If you want to be happily on top, accept that you deserve good stuff and are the only one who can provide it—by setting bound-aries and rejecting unacceptable behavior. Consider what you've done for others. Don't you deserve to be appreciated? Heidi says,

"Almost two years ago I discovered I'd been a scapegoat for almost every person involved in my life. I still give a lot but now know to feed myself first, over everything. I try to remember how I got here." Self first provides you a real self to give!

> **EXERCISE:** Keep a journal of things people do to you that you
>   don't like. Every time you find yourself angry about something
>   that was done to you, or how you were taken for granted,
> write it down, with the date. For each, answer:
>
> - Why do you think you let it happen?
> - Is it OK for it to happen again?
> - What might you do differently to prevent it from happening
> again?

Going to the Opposite Extreme—a Bitch

Bitches seem to get more. Anger can make you want that direction. I tried the bitch route but didn't like me. Stopping your pleasing ways doesn't mean being aggressive or unwilling to help others. Nice feels better says Yassmin:

> *If someone hurts me, I feel the urge for revenge but don't follow it. Being nice makes me happy and peaceful. It's part of human nature. When I please others, I feel pleased myself. When I give and receive, I reach the balance I yearn for. But I won't deal with selfish people.*

I'm very nice and treat everyone with respect. But I no longer give myself away. A middle ground feels better than being tough with everyone. Be nice with boundaries! Susan hated being nice since people took advantage of her good nature. She wanted to be a bitch and swore off being nice but hated herself that way. After my class she called to say she was back to being nice—a Nice Girl on Top—and said:

> *I'm setting limits and sticking to them. I feel more in control and happy to still be nice. I've finally accepted that people don't have to be nice to me and I don't have to give to someone who doesn't deserve it. I'm more at peace. It feels much better than being a bitch, and I'm getting a lot more in nice ways.*

 NOTE TO SELF: You can be nice and still get taken seriously.

Women have a reputation for going the bitch route at work. A tough, aggressive facade may help you get taken more seriously on some levels, but people won't like you. It's unnecessary. Prove yourself without getting tough. Janise says:

> *I got disgusted with being nice, toughened up and refused to take any crap. I was determined to get mine at work. I advanced and ran my office like a general. But there was no one to eat lunch with. Everyone kept a distance. I was lonely. This wasn't what I wanted. Before I bought friends, and now I scared them away. It took time to create a middle ground at work. I made new friends who know me as I am today—nice but firm and taking care of me while I help friends when I can. Being a Nice Girl on Top is much better than being a People Pleaser or a bitch.*

Bitchiness attracts less love. It's unnecessary to be aggressive or raise your voice to get taken seriously. Nice Girls on Top make a strong statement in a soft but firm way. Find a middle ground and enjoy the rewards of feeling nicely satisfied!

◞ Redefining Your Inner Nice Girl ◟

. . . .

*"You've got to make a conscious choice every day to
shed the old—whatever 'the old' means for you."*

—Sarah Ban Breathnach

Pay attention to how happy you are—or not! Decide whether
you want to transition into a Nice Girl on Top. She's in you! But-
terflies begin as caterpillars. It's hard to look at those creepy things
and believe they'll eventually be beautiful. Instead of continuing
behavior that makes you feel unworthy, spread your wings and
soar like a lovely butterfly. You *can* come out of your protective
cocoon and take control of your life.

Preparing to Fly

Start your path to becoming a Nice Girl on Top by accepting that
you're entitled to prioritize *your* needs. If you begin today, you're
one day closer! I'll help you get there. Work from the inside out.
Heidi did when she began to value herself:

> *I realized that in me is the God I was searching for. I am a daughter
> of the universe, and by valuing myself I contribute to the greater
> good. I set my worth, and when I demand that I treat myself with
> goodness and care, others who are out to hurt and control me will
> back off. I realized that after years of searching for someone to
> tell me I'm doing a good job. All it took was starting to tell that to
> myself and then allow the room to value myself. Then the real work
> began.*

Self-awareness leads to growth. As Heidi paid attention to herself and accepted her right to be happy, she began to believe it. Each
bit of self-realization is a step toward valuing yourself. Set small

boundaries as you inch forward. Ask, "Do I get what I want from
those I support?" Be honest! You can't tackle a problem before recognizing it. Michelle worked hard on self-awareness:

> *I really investigated why I behaved as I did. Seeing how your pat-*
> *terns don't work for you is often the first major step toward chang-*
> *ing them. I realized that I let people walk all over me because I*
> *lacked self-love and believed nobody would like me if I didn't. I then*
> *realized I was seeking acceptance to make me happy but I wasn't*
> *happy at all. By focusing on the happiness instead of the accep-*
> *tance, I started teaching myself (and am still teaching myself) to*
> *enjoy approving of myself as much as I appreciate gaining approval*
> *from others.*

Happiness is the best barometer of whether you should do
things differently. If you're happy pleasing everyone at your
expense, keep "welcome" on your butt. But since you're reading
this book, I assume you want to be happier. I think it's impossible
to be happy when giving is a one-way street and you're going the
wrong way. You might feel happy momentarily because of someone's gratitude. But that's not internal. If you often feel discontent,
pay attention and redefine your concept of Nice Girl.

Living for Today

Scars from past hurts shape your response to people and situations today. When I was fifteen, a guy said that with my pretty face
and good shape, I'd be a knockout if I lost weight. That sentenced
me to years of believing I had to please to compensate for being too
fat. It took years to accept I wasn't fat. All because a short, fat, slov-
enly guy said I wasn't good enough! Past experiences can keep you
as vulnerable as when they happened. Living now helps you check
mental suitcases and become empowered.

EXERCISE: Write down memories that contributed to insecurity—criticism, mistakes you're scared of repeating, abuse, or anything that lowered your self-esteem. Choose a quiet time and read it aloud. Then declare, "The past is over." Burn the list and consciously let go of old baggage.

Today is all that matters. When memories creep up, list what haunts you and say, "Today is a new beginning." You're not the person you were then! This is today! Why reinforce old limitations? Krista says:

When I heard that in class, I thought about how I dwelled on old stuff that made me believe I had to please everyone. I made the list over a month as I kept remembering more. Those things are over, but I kept them alive in my head. They kept me pleasing! When I burned my list, I felt like I had permission to begin over. It's a fresh day, and I'm choosing to take care of myself more, right now. It's taking a while, but I'm learning to focus on the present.

Something may not work out later, but it might. If you focus on right now, right now things are fine. It's harder to enjoy what you have if you focus on what could be. Do you fret that rain could ruin your barbecue tomorrow? Deal with it tomorrow *if* it rains. Why ruin today with what might not happen? The past and future aren't now. Living for the future postpones happiness indefinitely. Be happy now! Leave the past behind and live tomorrow when it comes.

Being Nicely on Top

I treat everyone with respect and consideration, enjoy helping when possible, and do my best to respect my own needs. I'm soft-spoken but express feelings and desires. Holding things in creates unhealthy anger. You're entitled to be important! Mala learned:

> *I'm much happier because I no longer agree to do things I don't want to do or feel I have to justify not wanting to do something. I'm happier because I listen to my intuition. When I'm not sure what I want to do, I tell people I'll get back to them. I'm also happier because I've broadened my perspective of being a nice girl. This allows me to appropriately express feelings of anger, disapproval, or disappointment without feeling like I'm a bad person.*

NOTE TO SELF: Avoiding confrontations and cutting people too much slack make things more peaceful and pleasant for all but you.

Don't do nice things for bargaining chips or succumb to guilt about not doing someone's bidding. You can effectively stand up and win, like Rayna:

> *I was brought up to be obedient. My role model—Mother—catered to everyone, saying that's what women did. So I pleased but always complained about how people took me for granted. I was miserable. When I expressed myself more, people balked. Mother said I was unladylike. Just because I told people I wasn't their go-to girl! I just had a daughter and won't teach her that* lady *means being a mat that others wipe their feet on. I've redefined* ladylike!

While I'm not immune to what people think, what I think of myself matters more. For now, affirm, "I am willing to try to release patterns that keep me from being self-empowered." When you believe it, use my tools to grow! Earlier Jen talked about a boyfriend who ignored her interests and dreams as she lost herself in the relationship. When she finally left, she vowed to stay strong. Jen explains:

I never want to be untrue to myself again. It's like feeling uncomfortable in your own skin. No one has a right to make me feel that way. It is that nightmare of feeling "not me" that motivates making myself and what I want a bigger priority. It is healthy to voice my opinion, and it should not only matter but also be respected. I've grown into a stronger woman because I know now I can rely on myself to make my goals a reality. I don't need to be with someone—there are other fish in the sea! Knowing I am finally in control of my life is something I've worked very hard to achieve since leaving my ex. I'm proud of my accomplishments, and the men I date now find my interests and goals fascinating! There is no shame in learning from mistakes.

3

Power Busters

―――――

**"And oftentimes excusing of a fault
Doth make the fault worse by the excuse."**

—SHAKESPEARE

*P*EOPLE PLEASERS USE strong defenses to avoid speaking up. They defend a disrespectful guy with bad behavior to friends who criticize him or find reasons to stay in People Pleaser ruts. When you recognize your People Pleaser habits, take action to break them.

No Excuse for Excuses

"Words are, of course, the most powerful drug used by mankind."

—RUDYARD KIPLING

"BUT . . . THIS IS different." "But . . . there's a good reason." There usually isn't, but People Pleasers accept any justification for unacceptable conduct when scared of losing someone. They prefer keeping their world stable, however unstable it really is. Do you defend actions that hurt and accept stinky excuses? Prepare to drop them!

Excuse Blinders

People Pleasers accept lame excuses and regurgitate them to friends who try to enlighten them. I've defended people to friends, my therapist, and others, knowing it sounded weak. But excuses just mask inexcusable behavior. Brenda said in class:

> *Finding reasons for why people hurt me was less painful than facing the truth. When Janie let me down regularly, I remembered her terrible memory and believed she meant well. I attributed Keith's mean sarcasm to problems with his mom. I excused everyone to avoid confrontations. Now I see I was better off without them. I've ditched most and am happier. But I can't find a good excuse for being stupid for so long!*

I reassured Brenda she wasn't stupid. The need to be liked, instilled in many females, drives us to wear blinders. But while excuses sugarcoat the truth, they don't change it. If you're afraid to challenge excuse makers, decipher what scares you:

- ▶ "Even if my boss is mean, I can't quit until my résumé is perfect" can mean "I'm scared to look for another job."
- ▶ "I can't get divorced until my kids are grown" can mean "A single man wouldn't want me with two kids."
- ▶ "I can't say no. My friend counts on me" can mean "I need to feel needed."
- ▶ "She doesn't mean to take advantage" can mean "I can't risk losing her."

Do any of these sound familiar? I accepted absurdly feeble excuses in my DoorMat days, rather than risk being alone. But I *was* alone, since I had no one to count on! Daylle was the go-to girl for favors, but people got scarce when I needed one. I'd have an "ouch" moment from the excuse, then convince myself it was true. Cheri related:

> *I'd help anyone. I needed people around until the cost got too high. Suzy asked for help at her home office. I didn't feel well, but she used guilt. At the post office, she'd forgotten her credit card, so I paid, though she already owed me from weeks before. The next day I was dizzy with a high fever and needed something at the drugstore. Yet everyone had excuses. Suzy was too tired. I finally snapped and registered for this class. No more excuses!*

 NOTE TO SELF: Nobody is perfect, but bits of good don't validate bad behavior!

Do you let one good facet of a person offset bad behavior? She doesn't keep her word *but* is fun to party with. He sponges off you *but* is affectionate. Excusing with *buts*—"I want better treatment or a respectful boss or support from friends, *but . . .* "—keeps you stuck. Stop settling for sweet crumbs thrown your way. Become aware of how often you excuse unacceptable behavior. Courtney shared in a class:

> *I was a "but" girl. I found reasons for not addressing what angered me. My cousin asked what I was scared of when I went into my umpteenth complaint about a friend. Me scared? Yes! She pushed me to analyze my justifications for letting friends off the hook. I was scared they'd leave if I spoke up. That "but she helped three years ago" has been repaid enough. And "but he encourages me" doesn't help my self-esteem as much as his nastiness hurts it. I slowly stopped allowing people to get away with troublesome things. My self-esteem is healing!*

EXERCISE: Create an excuse list and add to it whenever you use one, with the date. This intensifies awareness of Swiss cheese excuses. The holes become more apparent on paper.

Their Problems, Not Yours

We often use someone's legitimate problem as an excuse:

- ► "She's single, with three kids, and doesn't mean to talk down."
- ► "My boss yells, but he's under pressure."
- ► "She snaps a lot but has a hard life."
- ► "He doesn't follow through on his word, but he's working two jobs."
- ► "I shouldn't add to his problems even if it hurts me."

You're not responsible for people's problems or shortcomings. Let them take their baggage on a trip with someone else! If a friend gets PMS, ask for advance warning so it's your choice to see her. If he says, "I'm not always nice; take it or leave it," leave it. He's really saying "I won't change, so take my crap." Zoe shared:

> I accept a lot, but John had a rough childhood, and women before me treated him badly. He's still healing and tries sometimes, so I cut him slack and deal with painful stuff since I understand. It's hard for him to see me when he feels so lousy. He says my cheerfulness annoys him.

Is she wrong for being happy? A resounding *no!* Unhappy people resent happy ones and take advantage if allowed to. You don't owe them. Change your response to behavior you don't like and it may change. Otherwise, let the person wallow in his junk, alone. Don't let people use guilt to play you, Janice says:

When we met, Lamar explained his rough life. I tried to heal him with love but got verbal abuse when I evoked memories of someone who'd hurt him. He apologized after, promising to change. But our relationship was a seesaw—up when Lamar was loving; dropped hard when he soured. I was always on edge, waiting for mood swings. After hearing about his terrible family after more abuse, I screamed, "I'm not them! You need help!" and left.

People Pleasers can get used as verbal or physical punching bags to release frustration from someone's past. If you're consistently hurt, no excuse should excuse that! I've been there—given leeway and looked hard for excuses rather than deal with the bottom line: this person needed to be cut loose, or at least handled differently.

When Will We Learn?

"Experience keeps a dear school, yet fools will learn in no other."
—BENJAMIN FRANKLIN

UNHEALTHY SELF-DEFENSE MECHANISMS reinforce getting burned by allowing emotional pyromaniacs to take advantage of your need to be liked. Insecurity is manufactured in-house. Do you hate one trait that clouds your whole self-image? I remember when all I saw in the mirror was cellulite. It made me ignore my lovely qualities. Dave observes:

Many women are insecure about their looks, weight, eating habits, etc. It's kind of crazy in my opinion. Ultrathin women worry about their weight! It's actually a turnoff for me and many of my friends. I'd much rather be with a woman who is comfortable with and confident in her appearance and maybe isn't that ultraskinny, ste-

*reotypical, unrealistic supermodel weight, rather than a woman
who strives to be that and is never satisfied!*

Insecurity is the Krazy Glue of power busters, keeping you
stuck in pleasing mode and accepting inexcusable behavior. It
attracts unhealthy situations. Becoming a stronger person can
change that.

Apologitis

Do you apologize from habit? Have you said "I'm sorry" after
someone else goofed? People Pleasers equate apologizing with
being polite. Those words poured freely from me. I'd get kicked
and apologize! People Pleasers go overboard, just in case. Apology habits subconsciously reinforce guilt, which there's already too
much of! Have you said:

▶ "I'm sorry to bother you but must ask how you want this done."
  Why apologize for doing your job?
▶ "I'm sorry for not knowing you weren't in the mood for
  chicken instead of the steak I prepared." How could you know
  what he craves?

Each apology adds more guilt. Why be sorry for what you didn't
do or can't control? A waiter disappears. You wait for the check,
then say, "I'm sorry, but we need to leave." Hello! That's his job.
He delays you and gets "I'm sorry." A friend breaks a glass. You
apologize before she can. LaTonya says:

*I apologized for inane things for years. Mom blamed her problems
on me, so taking responsibility for everything bad became a habit.
Subconsciously, it reinforced my need to please—I always felt
wrong. When a co-worker spilled coffee on my desk and I apolo-*

gized, she asked, "Why are you sorry? I spilled it." That began my awareness. I began to stifle apologies unless one was truly merited. Now I rarely say "I'm sorry." It's amazing how much that's changed my attitude.

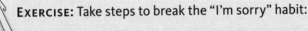

EXERCISE: Take steps to break the "I'm sorry" habit:

- Become conscious of when you apologize.
- Write down whom you say "I'm sorry" to and why. Each time.
- Identify reasons and objectively see which make sense.

Constant apologies reinforce feeling powerless. Think first. Is it warranted? If you're wrong, apologize for the specific action. Including a reason increases your awareness. Replace unnecessary apologies with other phrases:

- ► "I'm sorry you knocked the papers off my desk" can be "Oops." Let the paper knocker apologize.
- ► "I'm sorry I didn't buy skim milk" can be "It's a shame you didn't tell me."
- ► "I'm sorry you were in an accident" can be "I empathize with your pain."

Save "I'm sorry" for legit mistakes. Control apologitis by affirming "I did nothing wrong." Heidi finally learned, explaining:

When someone apologized for something there was no need to apologize for, I told her, "Don't apologize for something you didn't do or that has no bearing here." Then I took my own advice!

NOTE TO SELF: Apologizing on autopilot reinforces that everything is your fault.

I'm Sorry. Not!

Many people feel they can be hurtful, mean, or disrespectful as long as they say "I'm sorry." *Wrong!* It doesn't make unacceptable behavior OK. Words, often empty, are easy. Does "I'm sorry" heal bruises caused by an abusive man or erase hurtful deeds? It never did for me. Lisa told a group:

> *My friend Judy drove me crazy. She forgot plans, didn't return calls, and in general was unreliable. When I broached it, I got her automatic "I'm sorry." When she made an overt play for my date at a party, I was furious. Her empty apology was the final straw. I cut her off. I don't want a friend who thinks saying "I'm sorry" erases doing wrong. I want good actions!*

Lisa learned that how friends *act*, not what they say, is important. Hearing that, Margot said her boyfriend thought "I'm sorry" balanced hurtful actions and wised up:

> *Greg thought his insensitive actions were neutralized by apologies. I didn't feel better, but he did what he wanted. One night on the phone he yelled that his problems were my fault. I hung up. The next day he apologized profusely. I refused to accept it. Enough! I said don't call until he could consistently be respectful. He replied, "But I said I'm sorry." Why do people think that makes bad behavior okay? After I hung up more times, he got therapy. I'm seeing him again, on my terms. Wish I'd stopped accepting apologies sooner.*

Most folks are sorry after hurting you. Make them sorry enough not to repeat it. People are responsible for their actions. If they cause unhappiness, insist on positive actions, not words. If you excuse easily, people will hurt you easily. Forgiveness should be earned. Explain you accept their apology but not their behavior and you'll reserve judgment until you see future behavior. Sorry must be shown, not just said.

The Never Again/Usually Again Syndrome

Have you said "Never again!" after someone took advantage, but weakened? It's hard to keep resolutions. We repeat mistakes over and over, hoping it will get better. Have you loaned money to someone who already owes you? I hate asking for it back, like Gloria:

> *I was saving for my first vacation. My friend Cindy knew about my nest egg and regularly asked to borrow for some emergency. Not a lot, but she never repaid. I asked but got sob stories. I tried saying no, but she made me feel guilty. I gave in, ignoring her new clothes. Before booking my trip, I called to demand my money. Cindy was on vacation. I'm still saving, and she's still broke.*

NOTE TO SELF: When you say "Never again," mean it! Why should people keep their word if you can't keep your word to yourself?

Although she didn't get repaid, Gloria still loaned Cindy money, hoping she'd change. I'd hope for future change, but once a pattern is set, people expect acquiescence.

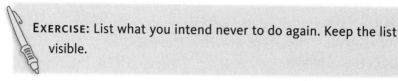

EXERCISE: List what you intend never to do again. Keep the list visible.

Emotional Baggage

. . . .

"When you control the ball, you control the score."

—PELÉ

YOUR POWER BEGINS inside. Until you control inner reactions, it's harder to control situations. Your control gets diminished if frustration, anger, impatience, and insecurity affect your response and outlook. Decide whether you want to take control or defer to whatever triggers anger or frustration. Your call!

Taking Charge of Emotions

Emotional situations can bring out the little girl in us. I believe we're conditioned early to use emotions to get our way. The more it works, the more it becomes a habit. It hurts in adulthood, but lifetime habits stick. Your response today may reflect yesterday's pain. Frustration triggers emotions that can make you feel out of control. Julie says:

> As a child my tantrums got me my way, so I continued, until I exploded at my cousin Michelle. She said I always scream to get my way but thinks I'm never content. It was true! I didn't know how to interact without emotions and felt out of control. Michelle said people avoided the drama I create. It was time to grow up. I'm trying to rein my emotions in.

When I began my record label, women execs warned I must keep emotions in check at all costs. They advised biting my lips and afterward releasing frustration in private and returning smiling confidently. Controlling emotions allows more control overall. It's your choice to go the drama route or take control. How?

▶ Be alert to what triggers emotions. Frustration? Anger? Not getting your way? Nerves? Catch yourself before losing control.

▶ Separate past hurts from present situations. Do hurtful memories trigger you to overreact? Be conscious of whether the anger you feel is at least partly saved up.

▶ Create inner self-talk—"I know I'm OK"—and use it over and over to conquer emotions.

▶ Practice addressing trigger situations in controlled ways.

▶ Consider what sparks emotional reactions and find calmer ways to deal.

▶ Take your time and breathe deeply.

▶ Silently count to fifteen to reclaim some control.

▶ Smile. You'll look and feel better.

Untamed emotions foil good results. Do you get dramatic about problems or take frustration out on others? Nicely but firmly asserting your point, *sans* emotions, is more productive. Elise learned after many calls to her wireless company:

> *Each time I called, frustration made me louder. They'd ask me to calm down, but I yelled and got nowhere. You asked if I'd like being spoken to that way. No! I called again, spoke nicely, and heard the difference in how she listened. It made her want to help. And she did! Now I try to control emotions. They get me nowhere but more emotional.*

Try to control impulses to play situations out emotionally. Get enough sleep. A better mood helps you brush off agitation triggers. If someone upsets you, excuse yourself. Courtney says:

> When my emotions ruled me, I hated myself. When I met Jilli, I envied her unruffled manner. One day everything went wrong, yet Jilli calmly juggled. I asked how. She said she likes feeling in control and intentionally manages her emotions. And she boxes to relieve stress. I've joined her and punch out frustrations. That helps control my emotions. The more I control, the more empowered I feel!

Exercise can be calming. Put situations that fuel emotions into perspective. If you feel emotions rise, pinch yourself. Controlling emotions when possible is a big power booster.

Trading Anger for Power

People Pleasers think anger isn't nice. Smiling and suppressing behind an acquiescent facade seems more agreeable. Women I've counseled say they're not angry, but I hear it—not overtly, but a stifled irritation that makes them whine or sound hard. At first they deny it. But when I point out specifics and offer reassurance, they own it. Jessie says:

> I'd push anger away or scream, which felt good momentarily but left me ashamed after. The person didn't understand why I was angry and got annoyed. I experimented. Nicely explaining myself feels in control, and the person listens objectively. Knowing I've

made my point helps me let it go. I feel free now. I control the anger instead of its controlling me.

Set yourself free! Articulate anger in a nice but resolute way. People Pleasers are subtle—sarcastic, talking behind backs, or getting even. Like steam, anger needs outlets. Outbursts don't resolve problems, especially if you're angry with yourself for allowing things to happen. Michelle shares:

There was a consistent struggle between the part of me that believed I was worth more than how people treated me and the other, less confident part that let it happen. These conflicting messages festered continual frustration. It wasn't so much people that made me angry. I was disappointed in myself for being in a position not to be taken more seriously. By focusing on feeling good about me, I'm now making decisions that change that dynamic.

EXERCISE: Write down everything you're angry about—past and present—and how it makes you feel. Ask yourself, "Am I willing to let go of anger or continue suffering?"

Do you replay scenarios in your head to tell someone off later or avoid repeating mistakes? Writing transfers anger from inside you to paper. I'd lie awake, imagining how to tell someone off. One sleepless night, I wrote down my thoughts. As more emerged, I wrote again. Then I slept. Tuck your list into a drawer and stop actively stewing. When you pinpoint what makes you angry, calmly express it, even if it's uncomfortable. Getting it off your chest feels better. People associate releasing anger with screaming or getting emotional. Lose that concept! Anger can be effectively chucked softly. Use my communication tips in Chapter 8. And remember:

▶ Wait until you're calmer, not rushed.

▶ Address it fast and send it bye-bye.

▶ Be specific, *sans* melodrama. "I feel like you don't trust me when you ____" instead of "You hurt me when you ____."

▶ Avoid attack mode. It's harder to listen objectively if you yell. Keep a soft, level, and friendly tone.

▶ Don't use nasty words.

▶ Focus on actions or situations, not the person. If he didn't clean the garage as promised, be angry the garage isn't clean.

▶ Don't be apologetic. "I hate saying this" dilutes the point. Use a version of "I don't want anger to hurt our friendship, so I'll share this. . . ."

▶ If told your feelings are wrong, don't get defensive. State that you're entitled to them.

> **EXERCISE:** For serious anger, write a letter as if speaking. Include all your feelings. Read it out loud as if the person were there— with emotions. Then forgive the person and burn it. I watch my anger disappear and feel lighter after.

Anger hurts you, not the one you're angry with. You can break the habit of staying angry if you *choose* to. Take a deep breath and think happy thoughts. Heidi believes:

Holding on to anger makes me bitter and angry. It takes more energy to be those than the energy it would take to make fifteen people smile. I thought about the good and the bad wolf that is inside everyone—feed the good wolf and starve the bad wolf. Then I realized, love the bad wolf and eventually he will be a good wolf as well. That's where I'm at today.

Forgiving frees you from being a prisoner of resentment. Revenge doesn't. People eventually get theirs. Positive revenge is sweeter! Use the energy behind anger for good. My revenge—a career I love—is sweeter than hurting someone. Don't confuse forgive with forget. Forgive in your heart from afar. It's for you, not them. If Mom or a friend does something that embarrasses you under the guise of "helping," such as speaking for you with you right there or criticizing you in front of others, forgive inside and gently explain how it makes you feel. If someone does something unforgivable, forgive inside and move on. How do you forgive in your heart?

▶ Talk out feelings with friends. A friend's empathy feels better than fuming.
▶ Burn your feelings, as described earlier. Have a good cry if necessary.
▶ Think about your blessings.
▶ Consider how powerful you're becoming—it's your choice to forgive and let go.
▶ Affirm "I forgive [name]. It's over. I love myself and don't want to be angry."

Compassion enables forgiving. I live by the Dalai Lama's belief that people who hurt you are suffering. Happy people avoid unkindness. Replace anger with empathy for someone's pain. I've addressed mean behavior with "You must be hurt if you did that. I have compassion for you." It feels better than rage. Identify why someone may be hurting. Don't excuse it, but have compassion. Feel sorry for those who suffer enough to hurt others and grateful for your blessings and the person you are.

4

Nice Girls with Attitude

"Speak softly and carry a big stick."

—THEODORE ROOSEVELT

You can talk softly and carry a big stick—the conviction in your voice, the validity of your words, and a confident attitude. Speak nicely with a firm manner. Nice Girls on Top confuse people. We're nice, like People Pleasers, except our demeanors communicate an intention to get what we want. Yassmin says, "I always try to be nice, no matter what. That's how you make others feel guilty for not treating you right." Talking softly keeps the boat from rocking too hard as you shake things up. Be nice, soft-spoken, and as feminine as you like and get taken seriously by having your own big stick.

➷ The Real Silent Majority ➹

"To dare is to lose your footing momentarily.
To not dare is to lose yourself."

—SØREN KIERKEGAARD

Women have a history of keeping quiet and accepting the status quo. We complain to friends about job inequities but work hard.

We let men control relationships by making them too important. We accept unfair nonsense if we value being liked more than being respected.

Silent Permission

I let people take me for granted and shut my mouth when people I always supported ignored my needs. I laughed off disrespect and closed my eyes to poor treatment. My inability to communicate anger gave people the unspoken right to continue bad behavior. If you don't voice dissatisfaction, how can you get satisfied? Silence says you won't make a fuss. And while a fuss isn't necessary, speaking up is. Do you brood in silence rather than risk losing someone who does you wrong? LaTonya says:

> *I once laughed at myself after begging forgiveness from a man who'd hurt me but insisted it was my fault, though I'd done nothing wrong. Or I'd hug a friend who owed me money but pleaded poverty—as she shopped for clothes. I was so scared of loneliness that I sulked silently. Now I understand my silence told them to continue. After being mad that I had allowed it, I ditched the boyfriend and firmly gave my friend two weeks to pay. I'm determined to prevent more bad treatment. Being on my own is much better than being with someone who hurts me!*

 NOTE TO SELF: People continue to do what they get away with.

People fall into bad habits that your silence permits. Breaking bad habits takes consciousness. Emily learned with her roommate:

Laurie asked for rides regularly, like I owed her for not having a car. I hated it but felt guilty saying no. Laurie worked evenings, often called to pick her up, and slugged guilt if I declined. One snowy night I was scared to drive, but she pushed. That was it! I explained she had chosen to work evenings and it wasn't my responsibility. She's annoyed but accepts it. We're still cool. The power over that felt wonderful.

Some people without cars expect those with one to play chauffeur. Your response guides folks. What keeps your mouth shut? Silence gives people permission to continue what you don't like. The longer you let it slide, the harder it is to reverse it. Begin now!

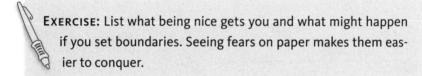

EXERCISE: List what being nice gets you and what might happen if you set boundaries. Seeing fears on paper makes them easier to conquer.

Ditching the Victim Mentality

Women moan, "Why do people use me?" And groan, "Why me?" And whine, "I'll never get what I want because ____." Fill in that blank with "because I allow myself to be a victim." People don't make you one. You volunteer. Robin says:

My mom has a "Woe is me" tone. She blames everyone for her being unhappy. I learned the role well. My friend Lorraine's exuberance for life accentuated how unhappy I was. I hated being a victim! By paying attention to my thoughts and making happier friends, I'm slowly climbing out of the black hole I've been in. As I accept that playing victim is my choice and take charge of my life, the sun shines on me more.

People Pleasers suffer like pros and complain about who did them wrong. But you get no points for suffering. None! *Nada!* Listen carefully. It's *your* choice to accept behavior or change it. If you're taught that confronting its source isn't nice, you suffer. This is poison! You deserve happiness! Asking "Why me?" when life isn't good reinforces victimhood. Focus your energy on how to change situations. Jodee does:

I have been through some really tough life experiences and don't give up. I don't say "can't," and I always turn things inside out to find other solutions. I am not afraid of not knowing and having to find out. There is something good in everything. I am always looking for the pony in the manure pile. Where there is a will there really is a way.

EXERCISE: List what makes you valuable.

Do you accept suffering as punishment for not "being good enough"? That destroys self-esteem! In my DoorMat days I nurtured suffering as a lifestyle. Now it's banned! Choose—adopt a victim mentality or change your response. Madison believed she deserved to suffer for being overweight. Feeling like a loser, she blamed it for all of her problems. After several sessions, she smiles more:

Victimhood was programmed. Mom never smiled and called me fat. When I actually thought about why I felt like a victim, it was a no-brainer that I didn't have to be one. I slowly did consciousness exercises to appreciate my good attributes and affirmations about not being a victim. I haven't completely stopped, but I'm on my way!

Don't give others power over you. "He makes me feel unattractive." It's your *choice* to feel unattractive! Your response determines whether you're a victim of hurtful words or a powerful chick. I know it's hard to begin. But deciding to ditch the victim role and stand up for *you* attracts better treatment and increases your self-respect. Jaydee says:

> *I did more work than anyone in my office but earned less. I handled everyone's problems while they got the credit and more money. I liked my job and kept quiet. A new manager noticed how hard I worked, asked why I hadn't been promoted, and encouraged me to recognize my worth. I listed everything I did and nicely, with confidence, told my boss I deserved a promotion. After reading my lists over and over, I felt it! He agreed. Now I'm office manager. No more victim!*

 NOTE TO SELF: People can't consistently do negative things unless you let them.

Relinquish self-pity and change your situation! Why stay a victim? Taking a stand makes people less likely to take advantage. *You* control how folks treat you. Complaining is a cop-out. Nobody uses someone who won't allow it.

Becoming Decisive

Women are notorious for having trouble making decisions. Are you scared of making poor choices? Were you reprimanded for mistakes while growing up? Do you worry about disappointing or inconveniencing someone? When you hesitate and hesitate, it pounds your confidence. Do you play mental ping-pong between what others may want you to choose and what you really want? Try Mara's method:

> *I get input from some choice people. I've narrowed that group down considerably. Now I generally know my decision before I begin asking around, but usually ask to see if anyone else is noticing something different. I generally go with my gut, though.*

Get advice from someone you respect. Trusting yourself takes practice. Inability to make decisions adds to feeling powerless. You *can* become more decisive:

▶ Identify what makes decisions tough.
▶ Don't dwell on worst-case scenarios.
▶ Ask, "Am I concerned about pleasing someone?"
▶ Picture both sides. List pros and cons of each.
▶ Don't blow the decision out of proportion or make any too important. Very little is do-or-die.
▶ Tap your intuition. First thoughts are often right.
▶ Do affirmations to boost confidence: "I trust myself to make a good choice."
▶ Distinguish between serious and frivolous. Decisions that impact work, health, and family need more thought than where to eat.
▶ Practice making small decisions. As you see the world doesn't implode, tackle more.
▶ Praise yourself for making a choice. "I did it and can do it again!" Be proud of conquering blocks.
▶ While making a tough decision, nod your head in agreement to reassure yourself and fight doubt.

You won't always make perfect choices, and it's OK. Do your best. Hesitating increases stress. If it's not the best choice, it's OK.

Accept that you can't know everything. You can't predict every outcome. Evaluate situations and decide based on known facts. That's the best you can do.

⚜ First Steps to Confidence ⚜

. . . .

*"Never bend your head. Hold it high. Look
the world straight in the eye."*

—Helen Keller

Confidence is learned. *Everyone* has fears and insecurities. But some create a confident facade. Beautiful young women at the top of their game share fears and self-loathing at my workshops and during counseling. Nobody feels perfect, but some folks magnify flaws. My class was stunned when Jennie, who was gorgeous, expressed how unattractive she felt:

> *You don't understand! My stomach has loose flab. Everyone says I'm pretty with a great body, but my ex-boyfriend picked on me to tighten my pooch. I work out often, but it's never good enough. I can't appreciate the rest of me until my stomach is flat. I'm self-conscious about it, which makes me insecure.*

Note to self: *Your* perception determines your self-image.

Jennie's obsession with old criticism shattered her confidence. Nobody saw what she did. People Pleasers dwell on negatives. Nice Girls on Top focus on good qualities and appear assured. René

Descartes said, "I think, therefore I am." Even if your confidence is shaky, fake it with the techniques that follow. Practice can make it real! "I think, therefore I am." Why see yourself as a wuss if you can act confident? I'm seen as a confident chick. But I still get nervous in new or important situations and force myself to approach strangers at events. Often the difference between a confident woman and you is consciously projecting a self-assured aura. Adopt one and only you'll know what's faked! As you convince others, you'll own it! One day you'll realize you're not acting. I speak from experience. It's glorious to grow into confidence.

It's in Your Head

Real confidence begins by controlling your thoughts. If they scream doubt, confidence will get caught in the starting gate. As you appreciate yourself more, it's easier. Emily says:

> *I grew up knowing what I wasn't—smart enough, thin enough, pretty enough. Believing you're never enough kills confidence. I assumed my faults glared at people and always sounded unsure. After noticing women I admired knock their faults, I realized we all do it. Slowly I thought about my good traits, and they replaced my demons. My confidence grew with self-appreciation.*

 NOTE TO SELF: Your intentions determine what happens to you.

If you expect people to treat you poorly, they probably will. If you assume a request for a raise will be rejected, prepare to budget. Expectations show in your attitude. It's hard to appear positive if you dwell on negatives. Control how thoughts add or detract from confidence:

▶ *Take responsibility for your thoughts.* It's *your* choice to adopt criticism as *your* perception. Allowing insecurity to rule your thoughts reflects in your behavior. Remember Eleanor Roosevelt's wise words—"Nobody can make you feel inferior without your consent." You *can* choose to brush off criticism.

▶ *Remember that no one is perfect or completely secure.* Stop holding yourself to higher standards than others. Pay attention when celebs like Nicole Kidman express insecurity. Ella says, "I felt inferior at work until co-workers discussed their self-doubts. None seem insecure. They advised me to pay more attention to what I do right. Slowly, my confidence is improving."

▶ *Be your own friend.* When you knock yourself, consider what you'd tell a friend who did that. Replace abusive thoughts with reassuring ones. Kira laughed at this suggestion but ended up delighted. "I thought it was silly. But imagining what I'd tell a friend who trashed herself like I did alerted me. I stop friends from being harsh and must be kinder to me." Even if you don't believe it yet, say, "I'm OK!"

▶ *Give self-pep talks.* Affirm in a mirror that you're good enough. Recite your positive qualities. Support *you* as you do others. Janise says, "Talking to myself got me more in touch with me. The more I encourage, the better I feel. When nervous, I repeat 'You can do it' until I calm down and get busy." When I need a confidence boost, I say, "I'm Daylle Deanna Schwartz and know I'm capable." It encourages the first step.

▶ *Repeat affirmations.* Affirm that you can do what you want, repeatedly, until it sticks. Alita says, "My voice quivered, sounding pathetic when I made suggestions at meetings. Now I repeat, 'I know what I'm doing' beforehand. I seem more sure of myself." Repeat a positive until you believe it! "I can do anything I choose."

▶ *Maintain a winning mentality.* Even if things don't go your way, let faith keep you strong. I've said out loud, "I know things don't look good right now but intend for it to work out." Expecting good things attracts them. When you're stronger inside, you can feel like a winner even if you're not winning yet. Robin says, "I used to let one bad incident make me a loser. Now I accept that I'm a strong, capable woman, even if I make mistakes or get misjudged." Think like a winner and let it show, despite circumstances.

▶ *Stop negative thoughts.* "I can't get taken seriously." "People won't like me if I stop favors." Override them with affirmations. "Everything will work out for my good." Janna says, "When I paid attention, I was shocked at the casual self-defeating thoughts I had. Now I try hard to be positive. It makes a big difference in my spirit."

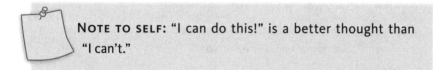

NOTE TO SELF: "I can do this!" is a better thought than "I can't."

▶ *Ask friends for reinforcement.* Invite pep talks about why you should be confident. Robin says, "When I couldn't get past my inner critic, my cousin listed why I'm terrific. My best friend pulled me in front of a mirror and made me praise myself. It slowly sank in."

▶ *Create a support team.* Buddy with someone who's also trying to improve. Talk every day—positively. Cheer each other on. Or create an informal group of women who meet to encourage each other. Call one when you're struggling. We benefit from helping each other.

It's in Your Voice

Your speaking manner makes an impact. Getting nervous, frustrated, angry, or insecure makes uncontrollable emotions creep into your voice. Hearing my annoyance or whining made me feel out of control. Leila relates:

> *I'm determined to sound confident, but my emotions get the best of me. When I feel insecure or a person isn't receptive, emotions ruin my delivery. I try to stifle them, and when they take over, I feel like a loser. Friends feel it too. Why can't women maintain control?*

 NOTE TO SELF: You can sound confident if you make a conscious effort.

The more you control emotions, the less they control you and the more confident you'll feel. Start by listening to yourself. Then use these tips:

▶ *Think before speaking.* Blurting things out fuels feeling out of control and feeling regret. Pause before responding. Say you'll think it over. Tamika says, "I always felt obligated to reply immediately. Then I'd beat myself up. Now I think first or say I'll let them know if I'm unsure. I feel more powerful." Thinking facilitates a controlled response, which increases confidence!

▶ *Speak with conviction.* You get taken more seriously if there's conviction in your message—a combo of how you phrase it and how assured you sound. Sounding like you're just hoping for instead of expecting a positive response doesn't come across as serious. "I'd like ＿＿. Can you get it for me?" can be "I expect to get the ＿＿. When will you have it?" Show you mean business! Being tentative or wishy-washy won't generate respect or results. Michael gives a guy's point of view:

> *Women need to act like women, not girls. In my office women complain they're not taken as seriously as men. But they don't take themselves seriously! One apologizes for everything she suggests. Another giggles when asking for things. Some prefer being flirty or cute. If they don't take themselves seriously, why should others? Women would get much further if they'd speak like they really mean it and leave female wiles for their personal lives.*

▶ *Use a gentle but firm tone.* People Pleasers speak timidly and get nowhere. Women at the opposite extreme are loud or tough, which annoys people. Nice Girls on Top have a friendly manner that also sounds firm about expecting results. Jessie says, "Nice got me nowhere, so I became aggressive. But that put people off. Now I speak nicely but sound resolute. People get the message." Speak softly but carry your big stick—a tone that says you're serious!

▶ *Take deep breaths before speaking.* Breathe deeply and release it slowly to calm down. Michelle says, "I speak quickly and get flustered when nervous or stressed. I make a special effort to breathe, take my time, and think about what I'm saying. I've seen results almost immediately."

▶ *Slow down.* When anxious, you may talk faster. Consciously slowing down and enunciating your words offers more control and allows leeway for speeding up if emotions kick in. Jennie says it calms her. "I used to be a motormouth. Blah, blah at high speed. It was hard to slow down, but as I did I felt control. People respond better. Now it's more natural." Managing your pace and enunciating controls emotions to help you feel more confident and sound more serious!

▶ *Bring your voice down an octave.* Does your voice go higher when you're frustrated or nervous? Emotions lower credibility if they make your voice squeaky. A quick fix? Begin speaking with your voice lower than usual to allow leeway when emotions make it rise. Women's voices tend to be higher than men's and carry less clout, even without emotions. Bringing the pitch down sounds more serious. And if you speak more slowly too, people will give your words more credibility. It translates into real confidence as you get better responses. Robin says:

> *I felt out of control when my voice got higher and then downright squeaky from nerves or trying too hard to make an important point. Like a domino effect, the more I tried, the more I sounded insecure and frustrated. A lower pitch helped control it. Now the domino effect is reversed. Modulating my voice makes me sound serious, which gives me real confidence!*

▶ *Tape yourself during phone conversations.* Listen back and pay attention to when your voice rises and speeds up. Become more conscious and slowly modulate your voice. The effort will prompt people to give what you say more credence, without your raising your voice!

It's in Your Body Language

Body language influences how you're viewed. Carrying yourself well enhances your impact. Have you seen someone enter a room like she owns it and assume she's confident? Why not show good presence? You can look secure while shaking inside! Force yourself to project confidence. These tips can mask insecurity.

▶ *Display good posture.* That's easy to fake! Standing tall is a good habit. Straightening your stance feels better physically. I initially developed good posture to avoid back pain and felt more confident by standing straight, arching my shoulders, and holding my head high. Your stance makes a statement. People will buy a confident image if you form good habits. Set a tone for their immediate perception of you. Good posture can make you look and feel more powerful! Tina related in a workshop:

> *I felt invisible at office meetings until my sister insisted I practice walking with my shoulders pulled back and head lifted. It was something I could do. At a recent meeting, people who had ignored me before asked if I was new and wanted to interact with me! The only new thing was my posture. Now it's automatic, and my confidence carries into other areas.*

▶ *Make eye contact.* It projects confidence and honesty. Looking down or away makes you seem unsure or untrustworthy. Shanna says, "I was scared of eye contact, so I looked everywhere else. When I force myself to do it, I get better responses." Eye contact makes you look self-assured and creates a connection.

▶ *Watch your movement.* Do you fidget? That shouts insecurity. Force yourself to be still. When seated, speak while leaning in toward the person. Don't cross your arms. Looking at ease makes you seem trustworthy. To make an important point, nod subtly like you're saying yes. It adds conviction.

▶ *Use a firm handshake.* A handshake sends a message. Limp ones don't impress. A firm handshake gets noticed. Practice your grip. Don't squeeze too hard, but let your hand seem confident, even if you're nervous. Jasmine says, "After practicing my handshake,

I feel more respect from people and I'm more confident for real now." A firm grip is easy to fake and makes a solid impression.

▶ *Dress for image.* Wear clothes that feel good and fit the image you want to convey. Notice how different styles feel. Jodee says, "In business I dress for the occasion and have a classic wardrobe available. I am never overstated unless I am speaking. Then I may wear clothing to make an impact." I don't like wearing makeup, but it enhances my appearance, which improves my confidence, so I wear it sometimes. Experiment to find what makes you feel good.

▶ *Exercise!* Working out does more than make you look better. Taking control of your body increases confidence. Five years ago I began weight training with a trainer. It was my first time in a gym and so hard I wanted to quit. But I didn't. Each session increased my self-esteem and intensified my confidence to try other things. Sheeda says, "I thought being overweight was my destiny. When I began power walking, I was surprised to lose weight. It motivated me to exercise more. Now I'm getting into good shape. I finally feel in control—powerful stuff!"

It's in Your Preparation!

Knowledge is a self-esteem booster. Preparation provides the confidence to pursue what you want. Acquiring knowledge and skills lightens the anxiety of trying new things and taking risks. Do you ignore your dreams due to insecurity? Learning counters that! When you feel inadequate, think about:

▶ What don't I know that could help me?
▶ How can I learn it?

NOTE TO SELF: The more new skills and knowledge, the stronger your confidence.

Find ways to improve what you perceive as inadequacies. Then stop lamenting why you can't do what you'd like. You can acquire more skills and knowledge. Set small and specific goals to prepare for pursuing desires. Jo said in a workshop:

I was brought up to be a housewife. After divorcing, I felt lost about technology. I told my kids I'd have to clean houses. They insisted I was smart and could learn skills. I enrolled in a computer class and enjoyed the enlightenment. I then hired the instructor for private lessons. When I applied for a job with no work experience, they doubted I'd fit in. But my confidence from my education impressed them enough to try me. I was just promoted!

When you pinpoint what you think you lack, change it:

▶ *Advance your education.* Do you feel inferior to co-workers? Learning provides a boost. Explore what might be valuable to study. What do co-workers lack that you could learn? To get promoted, take a class to learn what might help you shine as a candidate and increase confidence.

▶ *Learn a skill.* Are you tired of paying people to do what you could if you knew how? Do you want a better job or to paint? Learn skills! Adult ed classes and books teach people how to do a gazillion things. Learn to use watercolors, do simple plumbing, maintain a website, create a newsletter, and a lot more. You'll feel more competent.

▶ *Get a tutor.* Do computer classes go too fast or confuse you? Are you scared to take auto mechanics? Find an expert for private instructions. I'm dense at reading manuals and find people to explain, step by step. Computer whiz college kids helped for a few bucks. My friend gave me a guided tour under my car's hood. Find the right person to tutor you instead of feeling dumb about not understanding how to do it.

▶ *Read the paper.* Get familiar with current events. Many women ignore them. I did and felt insecure during discussions. Now I at least check the news on TV or radio to be armed with current knowledge.

▶ *Practice to become the best you can be.* Skills are like muscles. They improve with use. Decide what you'd like to do and practice. If it's painting, make time to paint! Learn a language? Find someone who speaks it and chat. You'll reach a higher level of competency by doing and doing. Be the best *you* can be. Forget perfection, or you'll never be good enough. Practice to improve.

▶ *Ask questions when you don't understand.* News flash! You're not the only one who doesn't always grasp instructions. People Pleasers nod in agreement and stressfully try to figure it out. Nice Girls on Top know that asking makes you smarter. Requesting more clarity doesn't make you look bad. "I'd appreciate your explaining that so I can get the whole picture" shows you're confident enough to ask. Insecure people don't. You can't know everything but can learn by asking.

The more you know, the less inadequate you feel. Nice Girls on Top try to get better at doing things. Stay ahead of the testosterone curve by educating yourself when you can! Jessie agrees:

As one of few female managers in my office, I'm watched more. So I give them something to watch! I pay attention to what's needed and read up on new technology. I've learned computer skills no one else has and read all journals related to my field to be more enlightened. I make innovative suggestions at meetings. Recently, six of us had lunch with an important client. He treated me differently from the men. I refused to feel like an outcast. When he mentioned recent advances in our field, we had a lively discussion of trends. I'd just read about it! The guys just sat there. The client recognized how knowledgeable I was and now wants to deal only with me.

Knowledge empowers!

✍ Good-Bye DoorMat Syndrome! ✍

"The last of the human freedoms is to choose one's attitudes."

—Viktor Frankl

It's TIME TO accept that *your* needs deserve priority in *your* decisions! This isn't selfish! Selfish folks do as they please. Nice Girls on Top evaluate each situation to decide what's best and do unto others when possible. Belinda told a group:

I'm a nice person who likes helping others. But I faced that I do it to count on them. I get angry when people turn me down, like they owe me. I recently started declining favors. That's a switch. I remind myself to help for the right reasons, not to cash in later. I'm more relaxed about my friends since I expect less.

Do nice things for other people if you want to be kind, not to buy friendship or favors. I like helping when I can but do it just for the sake of being nice. Heidi agrees. "It's nice to be nice. Always expect nothing in return from the person you help. If you expect nothing from the person you help, that's real help."

Nice Girls on Top Ask!

Most people won't give more than necessary. That's human nature. People Pleasers wait for people to offer and settle for what's given. Nice Girls on Top assume a right to ask for what they want! I dreaded asking until I realized that usually the worst outcome is being turned down. I can handle that. Mara, who's successful in marketing and sales, says she keeps asking until someone says yes, explaining:

> *I have this crazy streak in me that says you might as well try. I have one hundred ideas a day and am happy if I get ten actually going. I ask about all of them. It's a numbers game, I guess. Don't get me wrong; there are plenty of places where I get stopped. But I try to notice where and work through it or try something else.*

 NOTE TO SELF: You get little if you don't ask.

Do you assume you'll get turned down, so why bother? Don't block yourself! Second-guessing others loses big opportunities. Conquer fear of asking! Gillian, a writer, learned a valuable lesson when she got the nerve to ask for a job, explaining:

> *When I was breaking into writing, I met the publisher of a well-known celebrity magazine. I had little professional experience. Old voices warned me not to ask for a job. But I asked anyway and was hired as a reporter. After establishing myself, I asked the pub-*

lisher why she'd hired me. I'll never forget her answer: "Because you asked. Most people don't ask for things, which is a shame."

We're taught not to risk alienating others by asking for too much. Equal rights here, chickies! Men do it, so why not you? The more you ask, the more comfortable you get. Use the confidence boosters just described. Become conscious of asking more effectively:

▶ *Ask for what you need with conviction.* If you sound apologetic or unsure, people won't take your request seriously. Fake conviction! If you sound like you expect a bad response, you'll probably get one.

▶ *Beat the fear!* What's the worst that can happen? Someone says no? Remember—if you don't ask, no one will say yes. Heidi says she motivated herself to ask by driving straight through the fear. "The more it scared me, the more I did." It's OK to be scared, but ask anyway.

▶ *Be direct.* Don't drop hints and hope someone bites. State what you want clearly. If you hint and get ignored, you don't know if they understood or didn't want to do it.

▶ *Don't complain as a ploy for asking.* I was the master of wishful complaining—expressing unhappiness about needing something or how it's hard to find someone to help with _____. Be straight! "It will be hard to move on my own" can be "Can you help me move?"

▶ *Practice asking.* Start with small requests. Then try bigger ones. Heidi reassures, "The more you do it and know you come from a good place, the easier it gets."

▶ *Ask for and expect more.* This hasn't been an accepted mentality for women. But why not? Only asking for a little rarely gets you much. People aren't as used to women asking for lots. Get them used to it. Raise your expectations, which increases your chance of receiving more. More is better than less!

▶ *Affirm why you deserve what you're asking for.* Accept your right to receive! When she began asking, Heidi changed her attitude and says, "As I began feeding myself first, I realized I have a gift and am giving something completely that's worthy of what I'm asking for." Your attitude shouldn't reflect doubt. You're worthy of receiving!

▶ *Get into the habit of asking.* Learn from those who ask you. Why get requests from others and not make your own? Asking for what you want is a good habit to nurture! The more you receive, the more happy and confident you'll be.

EXERCISE: Write a few sentences that read like a sales pitch for what you want to ask for. Read it over and over. Then ask. Start with what feels like the least uncomfortable request and use each success to build confidence.

Starting Those Boundaries

Nice Girls on Top set clear boundaries—lines drawn that people recognize. Dancing around requests you want to turn down invites others. If you consider one, look in the mirror and say "Hello!" Why do it? Mala learned:

Once a friend planned to produce her first film. It was a big step for her, and as her friend I was encouraging and supportive. She asked me to assist with the project. I knew my schedule was already too busy. I was working full-time in an office, pursuing a career in music, and juggling my duties as a wife and mother. Still, I felt I couldn't say no—I was her friend and she needed me. When I failed to keep up with her needs, she became angry with me for letting her down. I felt frustrated and annoyed for my inability to say no in the first place. The final straw was when I couldn't make a meeting because I had plans with my husband and children. She commented that I already spent "too much" time with my family. We parted ways, but I knew I'd helped to create the problem. That motivated me to be more true to myself in making future commitments.

Think before agreeing to a favor. Say you'll check your schedule. People can't put you on the spot unless you allow them to. Evaluate each request by asking yourself:

▶ Will it take me out of my way or kill time I can't afford?
▶ Is it something I don't want to do?
▶ Will it make me complain later?
▶ Do I really want to help this person?
▶ Why should I feel obligated to agree?

Set your own terms for helping if it's not inconvenient. Create comfortable compromises. For example:

▶ If you help a friend move, don't stay all day. Choose an hour or two.
▶ Instead of taking a neighbor shopping, shop for her when you go.
▶ When asked for a ride, say you can drop her off at the closest point on your way.

- ► If your child enjoys playmates, allow a friend to leave her child for a period of time *you* set.
- ► If neighbors borrow things indefinitely, be clear about when they must be returned.

EXERCISE: Decide where to draw the line for how much you give others. List who asks for help in one of two columns:

1. Those who support you whether you do favors or not

2. Those who might disappear if you weren't their go-to person; who drain you, aren't good friends, or always give excuses or disappoint you

Be honest when you assess who deserves your help and who's not worth your time and energy. Friends in column 1 get priority; those in column 2 are at your convenience or not. Accept that you can't be there for everyone. "I deserve to be happy and give myself the time I need." Kayla learned:

When I made my list, there were people I didn't want to put in column 2. It was hard facing the truth about those I wished were friends. Soul-searching helped me identify most people as "friends probably bought with favors." As I did less, they got scarce. I was pleased when one got moved to column 1. Another asks for less. Learning to say no and assert my desires helped me identify true friends. I thought I'd hate having fewer friends, but instead I appreciate my real ones more.

The more you take care of you, the more you can give. Hustling to please everyone is draining. A good balance between helping others and time for you feels better. Don't get nasty to those in column 2 or stop favors. You won't like yourself! Just be more selective about what you can do. Michelle agrees:

> *I've learned the difference between people who give energy and offer support and people who drain energy and need constant attention. I am now prepared to give energy to people who give energy back and also help themselves. I spend less time with people who drain me without offering anything in return.*

NOTE TO SELF: Nice Girls on Top expect positive outcomes.

Being a victim is *your* choice. Trade self-pity for determination by paying attention to the good going on. Choose a negative attitude and be unhappy or choose to enjoy life. No one can ruin your day unless you let it happen. Dwelling on negatives improves nothing. Moving forward with a positive outlook does. Nice Girls on Top smile more. You can too! Jenn, in her early thirties now, found her way:

> *Aside from genuinely being an honest and caring person, I am hopeful and always give people the benefit of the doubt. That, in retrospect, was to a fault when at times I was taken advantage of, personally and professionally. It pains me even now to think of when I failed to open my mouth to stand up for myself. The older I get, the more I don't care about what people think. I went through experiences, and little by little I became more assertive and more confident. The more I stood up for myself, the easier it got, as with most learned behavior. Some people learn early on, but during those years I was on the defensive. Eventually I had to grow up.*

5

Finding Your
Inner Bitch

"In spite of everything, I still believe that
everybody is good at heart."

—ANNE FRANK

SOME WOMEN WHINE a version of "Why do people take advantage of me or not support me back?" My answer is simple: they don't have to! Most folks are good at heart, with reasons for being less kind than you'd like. If you accept the reality of how people are, you can change your response and be happier.

✍ To Deal or Not to Deal ✍

"Have no friends not equal to yourself."

—CONFUCIUS

STUDIES SHOW THAT people with good friends live longer. Seek people to be with—people you want to emulate, not avoid; who bring harmony, not drama. Clean toxic ones out. When you pay attention, you'll know who they are.

If You're Called a Bitch, Say "Thank You!"

You do things to get taken seriously. Nobody responds, so you get firmer. You've done nothing mean and speak in a soft, considerate tone. So it's a shock to be called something that's not nice. Word darts are weapons to make you return to more giving ways. Don't let names used to return you to *pleasing* mode stop your progress! You may be called:

- ▶ *Selfish:* People who call you selfish are the selfish ones for trying to make you do more for them. You're entitled to care for you.
- ▶ *A bitch:* People say it to manipulate you back to submission. Saying no isn't bitchy! Nor is having no time for favors, not loaning money, etc.
- ▶ *Aggressive:* Men are go-getters for taking charge. But it's not as easily accepted in women. Straighten your critics out, nicely.
- ▶ *Acting unfeminine for speaking up: Feminine* doesn't mean "wimpy"!

Being assertive in a nice, diplomatic way frustrates people who use ouch words unfairly. I've been called a bitch for expressing my opinion, holding firm to a decision, and winning in business. Leslie told my class how her hospital staff acted:

> *I'm a nursing supervisor. People goof off, making it harder on the rest of us. I tried friendliness, to be liked. Everyone walked over me, laughing when I tried pushing them. After getting tougher, I was shocked to hear "bitch" whispered. I wanted to hide. I'm nice, not a bitch! So I stopped pushing. Our floor is still inefficient.*

NOTE TO SELF: Names hurt you only if *you* accept them as true.

Letting words affect your behavior allows name callers to control you. Leslie's co-workers hindered her doing her job effectively by calling her a bitch. She called weeks later:

> *I accept that my staff uses* bitch *to stop my efforts to improve work habits. Now things get done* my *way. It hasn't been easy, and I've heard "bitch" again but no longer care. The patients get better care, and I'm fair. That's being a good supervisor! I'm getting grudging respect!*

As long as you respect yourself, and aren't nasty or purposely hurtful, keep going! Stay the course that name callers try to divert you from. Being called names signals progress. Just remember your manners and say "Thank you!"

Friends to Cut Loose

People Pleasers befriend everyone. Nice Girls on Top are selective. No one is exempt from good behavior! Take a stand—softly—on what you don't like. Robin agrees:

> *Mark was a decent guy, except for occasional biting comments. I complained to a mutual friend, who giggled, saying, "That's just Mark's way." Everyone disregarded it. Next time he called I refused to make plans because of his barbs. Mark laughed. I explained that, while others accept it, not me. Period! Guess what? Mark apologized and promised never to do it again to me—and didn't.*

As your self-respect increases, so will your standards for friendships and other relationships. Don't take words too seriously until there's action behind them. Just because someone has good intentions does not mean you have to suffer through regular cancellations, disappointments, and underhanded statements. Yassmin agrees:

I value friendship a lot. But there's no reason for one anymore if there's no more trust. To build a balanced and healthy relationship, people have to be positive, not holding you back and passive. I give energy to people who respond well. Friendship is like a seed—it needs care and time to grow.

EXERCISE: List the qualities most important to you in friends, like honesty and reliability. Then list those you've tolerated that consistently annoy you. Keep them handy to reinforce decisions about which friends to give priority and which new ones to cultivate.

Even if you've known someone for ages, lose friends who bring no joy and are always negative. As I cut down on time spent with these types or let go completely, I say "Close one door and another opens." Then new and more lighthearted and spiritual people enter my life. Letting go hurts initially but is positive. Mala explains:

When I cut off friends who need too much, or who don't treat me well, I always go through kind of a grieving period. I mourn the parts of the friendship that felt good, but know deep down that letting it go is the best thing. I've noticed that I'm getting better at recognizing potential problems a lot sooner. I'm also attracting healthier friendships as a result, and that feels great.

If someone regularly does things that greatly bother you, snip them loose, or limit contact. Determine what's an annoying quirk and what's unacceptable. Don't feel obligated to remain friends with people who aren't healthy for you. There are good reasons to drop someone or set boundaries:

▶ *You've outgrown her.* Your friendship revolves around old habits, like getting drunk. If you have only bad habits in common, break them. Suggest new activities. If she refuses, leave her in the past with old habits.

▶ *She needs to feel needed.* Some friends prefer you unhappy. They may be threatened and try to sabotage your growth. Snip.

▶ *She drains you.* Does a friend moan and groan as a lifestyle? If she can't find anything positive ever, pull the plug and let her take someone else down the drain.

▶ *She's overly demanding.* A friend who constantly whines "You don't make enough time for me" is a burden. You avoid her for a reason. Make it permanent!

▶ *You're her repairwoman.* She asks advice for everything and leans on you like a primary relationship or therapist and doesn't reciprocate. Cut!

▶ *She's insincere.* Some people talk big with no intention of follow-through. Maybe they need to be liked at that moment. Do not tolerate this behavior.

▶ *She's critical or unsupportive.* Do I need to elaborate on this? Bye-bye!

☙ Removing the Rose-Colored ❧ Glasses

. . . .

"Ye shall know the truth and the truth shall make you free."
—JOHN 8:13

REALITY GETS FILTERED through rose-colored glasses if you're not ready to face it. When I accepted that I had to respond to people differently, I became *much* happier. You too can pry off your blinders and find contentment in being nicely on top.

Adding Respect to Your Vocabulary

When I was on "Oprah," audience members discussed how much they please other people to be liked. But do they strive for respect? No! Many thought you couldn't be liked *and* respected; however, you can, by earning respect first. Emily learned:

> *I was taught that people like nice girls more. Being insecure, I inconvenienced myself for other people's convenience, despite not receiving—until my brother asked how I could live without self-respect. I was defensive, but he said people referred to me as a wimp. I indignantly said respect is for guys but paid attention. I noticed less acquiescent women get better treatment and asked my brother for pointers. Now I value respect and get it. And most people still like me!*

NOTE TO SELF: A nice person whose behavior commands respect is more sincerely liked than one who keeps friends by being agreeable.

Do you associate respect with alienating people? *Au contraire*, respected women get more! Respect is another aspect of developing self-esteem that most girls are not taught, so when they grow up they don't know how to earn it.

Respect yourself enough to stop letting people play on your kindness! LaTonya says:

> Respect *made me cringe. I associated it with rules and being unfeminine. My parents, who weren't nice, insisted on respect and*

insisted I be nice since I wasn't pretty. I hated myself for giving so much but was scared to change until I turned to God. I wanted to be a real good person. So I said no sometimes, helped if possible, and redefined respect as honoring me as a valued person. I'm a child of God and deserve it! Now that I respect me, others do too.

What's more important: being liked by others or by yourself?

Reality Sunshine

Learning to accept people, glitches and all, and changing your response to what you don't like empowers you. People don't have to act *your* way. *That's reality.* I hear women say things like "I can't believe she _____. If it were me, I'd do _____." But they're not you. *That's reality.* I hear:

- ▶ "I'd take her to the doctor if she asked. How can she turn me down?"
- ▶ "How hard is it to return a phone call? I make time."
- ▶ "Why can't people be nice back?"
- ▶ "I try hard to keep my word. Why can't others?"

Reacting differently doesn't make them wrong or bad. Follow my reality training: *if you want to be happy, accept people as they are and learn to interact with them as they are.* Everyone has good qualities and not so good ones. It's your choice to accept qualities that are annoying to you; however, you also have behaviors that may be annoying to others and it is important to keep an open mind. *That's reality.* People won't change because you want them to. *You* must change your response instead of trying to change them. It's *your* choice to tolerate or walk away from bothersome behavior. Molly was frustrated that her boyfriend always made last-minute weekend plans. She moaned while he did as he pleased. I explained she must stop complaining and respond differently. Molly says:

> *I finally recognized I had to accept Jared's ways and that I didn't have to be free when he was, and I made plans with friends. When Jared called Thursday about seeing a movie on Friday, I nicely said I had plans, without details, since he offers none. He thought I was joking and then asked if I was mad. Nope! He heard me smiling. I explained that since he does his thing, I'm doing mine. Jared got defensive, saying he's not used to advance plans. I sweetly said I'm not used to turning down friends in case my boyfriend calls. I accept his ways. He must accept mine. That leveled the playing field. I feel in control. Jared called next time on Tuesday. I expressed pleasure. Slowly he's coming around. Accepting his rights helped me change and get more of what I want.*

 NOTE TO SELF: If you want to be happy, accept people's right to their ways. If you can't—leave!

Adjust your expectations. What seems wrong can be right to someone else. There is always more than one way of doing something, so be less judgmental. If something feels unacceptable, look at it from the other person's shoes and change your response to it instead of getting angry. Being self-righteous about behavior you disagree with creates unnecessary anger. Robin says:

> *I always made a point of treating others as I want to be treated. Not receiving that consideration made me angry. My lectures about good behavior fell on deaf ears—until I indignantly told Sara that I call when I'm running late yet she didn't. She demanded I step*

back. I want to be Ms. Perfect, but she's not me. She said I complained a lot about people not doing things my way and advised lightening up since anger kept me unhappy. Now I accept people more. It's my choice to try hard. I'm more relaxed, less angry.

Once I accepted reality, I told a friend who was always late, "Meet me at my place so I can work while I wait." She did. Another friend rarely kept plans. He felt insulted when I wouldn't commit to joining him for an event. I explained I couldn't take it seriously since he usually bailed. I accepted his way, but he needed to accept that I won't keep time open since things rarely pan out. He swore he'd keep his word and did. All because I accepted him and changed my response! *People respond better to actions than complaints.*

NOTE TO SELF: Doing things for others doesn't obligate them to help you.

Accept the reality of people in your life. You can *know* but not *accept* it. Stop denying and fantasizing about how life should be. Everyone *should* be considerate, but that's not reality. Don't lose your good nature; change your attitude and how you react to unacceptable behavior if you want inner peace. It feels much better than complaining.

EXERCISE: When someone makes you angry, write it down. Take a few minutes to think about that person's behaviors: actions or habits that annoy you. What thought, reaction, or behavior could you change to avoid getting angry in the future?

✌ Your Wake-Up Call ✌

....

"That you may retain your self-respect, it is better to displease the people by doing what you know is right, than to temporarily please them by doing what you know is wrong."

—William J. H. Boetcker

You must set people straight. If someone screws you once, they may screw you twice. If they're still screwing you after two times, you're screwing yourself. Take control!

The Power Word: Responsibility

In my DoorMat days, I complained incessantly. Then I realized my response to people gave them permission to do as they pleased. It was up to me to stop it! Taking responsibility gave me the power to change my whole life. Mara says:

> *Taking responsibility for my own life means I'm the source of everything that happens, good or bad. If something is not going my way, I look at what I'm doing that is making it not go my way and change that. I don't feel like a victim. It's empowering!*

 Note to self: People can't do anything to you that you don't allow!

　　The core of self-empowerment is taking responsibility for how you're treated. *You* choose what to accept. *You* are responsible for how people view you. Once when I was doing volunteer work, I complained frequently about always having to pick up the slack for what others committed to do but didn't. My complaints were ignored. So I changed. I didn't have to do what others dropped the ball on. When someone said that she couldn't get something done, I would say, "Oh well" instead of "I'll do it." I got disbelief, since I'd always jumped in to help before. Now I consider how to change my response when a situation feels wrong. Complaining that people use you is a cop-out. Nobody uses someone who doesn't allow it.

Estelle says, "The turning point for me was happening upon Eleanor Roosevelt's quote: 'No one can make you feel inferior without your consent.' That was a lightning bolt for me." Taking responsibility dissolved my anger. I accepted that I could allow or change unacceptable stuff. Your power lies in accepting that *you*, not others, must change. People get cues from you. It's *your* choice to allow unacceptable behavior or stop it. Lisa in my support group learned:

Dating Tim was wonderful at first. Then he took me for granted, calling late, never bringing flowers, and showing little affection. I nagged incessantly, but he didn't change. You encouraged taking responsibility for accepting Tim's behavior. So I made plans with friends, bought myself flowers, decreased affection, and stopped complaining! Tim voluntarily changed. Later he admitted being scared by my newfound self-control and chose compromise over losing me. If he returns to his old ways, I return to mine. He learns without my saying a word.

EXERCISE: Stay conscious of unacceptable behavior with a rubber band on your wrist. Snap it whenever you allow yourself to be treated poorly, even by *you*.

Focus on changing your behavior instead of pointing fingers. *You* are why people treat you as they do. People take without giving, withhold respect, take you for granted, and are hurtful *only* if you let them! Nasrin says:

Taking responsibility for my life means to feel responsible for whatever happens in it, good or bad. I used to blame others for unpleasant situations, but now I truly believe that I have roles in my life and many things depend on my attitude and my decisions. I've learned to seek reasons within me and not to take bad things out on others.

Celebrate your power and practice using it in satisfying ways. Take responsibility and kick victimhood in the butt. Once you respond differently, people will see your power. Feeling powerless won't be an excuse!

Chuck Guilt!

We all feel guilty sometimes. But constant guilt eats you like rust on metal. At first rust discolors, but eventually it breaks down the surface. If allowed to continue, it spreads and makes holes. Guilt does that to your self-esteem when you let others determine what's right and wrong. In my DoorMat days, I rarely knew my "crime," but if something went wrong or someone criticized my choice, I assumed fault. Many of us are conditioned to feel responsible for the displeasure of others. Mala learned:

In the beginning I saw that my tendency to feel guilty made me an easy target for manipulation. I decided to do what was best for me and acknowledge to myself that I'd probably feel guilty and that it was OK to feel that way. At first I had to almost literally bite my tongue to stop myself from giving in to demands, but eventually it got easier.

Put guilt into perspective. Making a mistake (or three) doesn't justify beating yourself up with guilt. Accepting blame for something gone bad hurts you. Feeling wrong feels awful. If you purposely hurt someone, guilt might be warranted for a limited time. But feeling guilty as a lifestyle tarnishes happiness. Zita says:

When I was a People Pleaser, I was always guilty of not being a perfect friend, daughter, employee, etc. People manipulated me with guilt. Mom felt worse if I didn't call often. How could I think about lunch with so much work? If I grabbed a bite, I'd feel guilty. My sister asked what crime I committed by eating or not being Supergirl. I had no rational answers. Listening to my silly excuses woke me. I don't want guilt from not doing what someone else wants. Now I ask myself if I'm wrong instead of assuming blame!

Be careful. Guilt throwers are manipulative. Be objective about whether it's justified. Guilt makes your perspective less important than someone else's. You don't have to accept what others decide you should or shouldn't do. Michelle says:

I used to feel guilty about saying no, leaving work on time, not accepting duties at work that were not my responsibility, and going out without my boyfriend when he didn't have plans. I expected more from myself than from anyone else. Now I ask myself, "If the roles were reversed, would I be upset?" Often the answer is no. If I'd have no problem with someone else taking that action, I feel I can expect the same courtesy. If that action or decision would upset me, it's possible I need to reevaluate my thinking.

Don't accept unfair guilt. Why punish yourself for not being what someone else wants? Taking care of you is *not* wrong! Reframe what you did. For example:

► "I feel guilty not helping her" can be "I'd help but have no time."
► "I let my friend down" can be "I wanted to help but can't do everything."
► "I broke his heart" can be "There's no easy way to break up, and I had to."
► "I couldn't give what he needed" can be "I can only do my best."

If you're blamed for someone's troubles, evaluate whether you realistically deserve it. Be honest: is guilt warranted? Change your perception of a situation. If someone lays on guilt, remember you're a good person who can't do it all. Guilt is self-punishment. Love yourself enough to skip that! If you feel guilt brewing, ask:

► "Did I purposely hurt them?" If you didn't, why feel guilty? Not doing favors doesn't make you wrong or bad.
► "Was what I did in my best interest?" Often people prefer what's in their best interest. But taking care of self is your right.
► "Did I try my best?" If that's not enough, oh well. You can't be everything.
► "Was I truly wrong, or is someone manipulating me?" Selfish people rush to call others selfish—to guilt them into submission. Be objective.
► "Have I done something that warrants ruining my day with guilt?" Did you purposely hurt someone? If your intentions were good, there's no need to suffer for being imperfect in someone else's eyes. Let it go!

You must take care of you. When something stokes the ol' guilt vibes, put it into perspective:

► Feel bad that it happened for the moment.
► Apologize if necessary.
► Forgive yourself for being human.
► Let it go.

Stopping guilt in its tracks is a loving act that makes *your* view most important. If you see no fault, affirm, "I did nothing wrong and shouldn't feel guilty." Accept that you're a good person and don't owe everybody what *they'd* like. Let guilt take a backseat to self-love to keep your happiness strong. Naomi does:

> *I know that life is a precious gift, not a dress rehearsal, and that the people in my life who love and support me will do so knowing that the choices I make are done with the intended purpose of pursuing my happiness, health, and success.*

6

Baby-Steppin' New Habits

"It is not the strongest of the species that survive, nor the most intelligent, but the one most responsive to change."

—CHARLES DARWIN

OES THE IDEA of change unnerve you or seem overwhelming? Instead, try to focus on the benefits of handling situations in more satisfying ways—better than complaining without results. One constructive baby step at a time makes changing easier.

Personal Consciousness-Raising

"Take the first step in faith. You don't have to see the whole staircase; just take the first step."

—MARTIN LUTHER KING JR.

REMEMBER HOW LOUSY it feels to be treated in ways that are unfair or hurtful to motivate yourself. Change is a learning process. Accept that it's essential to your well-being.

Changing Your Perception of Change

Instead of seeing it as major overhauls, perceive change as an accumulation of small lessons used effectively to break old habits—not who you are. A Nice Girl on Top is the same person in a different package—a kind woman responding to situations more effectively. Zita says:

> *I used to think of change as too hard. Work. Risky. I felt like garbage and thought nothing could help. But I was wrong. I paid attention to how my need to be liked caused my problems—making me accept hurtful conduct from people who preyed on my desperation for approval. I slowly broke habits that pounded my self-esteem, like trashing myself to others. It's ongoing, but I'm happier already. Breaking habits felt easier than changing who I am. I still want to be nice!*

When you've always done something one way, it becomes a habit. And habits can be broken. That feels much more doable than a psychological makeover. Most of what you do, or don't do, can be replaced with healthier habits.

Kicking Your Own Butt

How many books or classes will it take to implement what you learn? It's easy to get knowledge but harder to apply it. Don't rush! Just take the first step. Each small one takes you a little higher. Take the first step, then another. If I did it, anyone can!

 NOTE TO SELF: To achieve what you say you want, be willing to do what it takes to break old habits. Are you willing?

Most people would change if a fairy sprinkled magic dust and said, "Poof! You're self-empowered." Oh well. Life isn't a fairy tale. Breaking tough habits requires a desire strong enough to give them up. Many people wait for miracles. They don't want it enough to do what it takes. LaTonya didn't:

> *I wanted people to take me more seriously. I'd complain, hoping to miraculously get stronger. Whenever I almost took action, fear made me wait for next time. And next time. Kendra got exasperated and said I just liked complaining. It got me thinking. I'm trying to stop postponing positive steps by recalling how friends hurt me. I'm ready!*

If people who say they want to slim down did it, talking about losing weight wouldn't be a national pastime. But people don't lose what they complain about. They prefer to eat junk and dodge exercise. If the fairy helped, we'd all be slim. But give up favorite foods? Not easily! When I wanted to lose weight more than anything, I changed my eating and exercise habits. If you want to be a nice girl who finishes first, nurture a desire that's strong enough to take action—to value yourself over the "security" of pleasing. It's worth it! Why wait for the self-disgust to build as Robin did?

> *I swear, God sent angels to wake me. I felt disrespected by friends I treated well, but I excused them. Two caring friends intervened. Lou yelled that I deserved better, and Kim scolded me for being used, saying I'm a wonderful person and should demand what I deserved. Yes, I finally decided I deserved good treatment, enough to change my habits! I absolutely want respect.*

Think about all you do. Don't you deserve good treatment too? Accepting that I deserved better woke me up and moved me—at last!

EXERCISE: List all the favors you've done in the last month and any unfair or disrespectful behavior you've tolerated. Then ask yourself, "Don't I *deserve* to be treated well too?"

Watching Small Change Add Up

You can't climb a mountain without the first step and then the second. Looking up may make the incline seem daunting, but each step takes you closer to the peak. When I climbed my first, going even halfway seemed impossible. But each step led to another. Reaching each ridge motivated me more. Confucius said, "A journey of a thousand miles begins with a single step." Take the first! Then another. Do small things differently. It may feel wobbly. Just as dieters regain weight, we get pressure to "be nice." Keep your resolve strong. Practicing each day strengthens me as I feed on the satisfaction of progress. As when building something, you need a foundation. Baby steps create one for a happier self:

▶ *Acknowledge that you need to change.* The hardest step may be ending the delusion that helping others compensates for your dissatisfaction.
▶ *Decide you want to change.* Make a conscious decision to seek more effective ways to handle irritating situations.
▶ *Pinpoint what to change.* Pay attention to habits. Assess which need breaking.
▶ *Decide what to change first.* Pick one person or situation to start with.
▶ *Try different techniques.* As with shopping, try on different suits until one fits properly. You may need different attitudes with different people.

- ▶ *Motivate yourself.* Let painful memories inspire handling yourself differently.
- ▶ *Consciously applaud progress.* Don't wait for major breakthroughs. Celebrate each baby step as an accomplishment, however insignificant it seems.
- ▶ *Be patient.* Empowerment won't develop overnight. It takes time to get comfortable with a new approach.
- ▶ *Activate receive mode.* Ask for help and accept it when offered. You do plenty! Expect support too.

 NOTE TO SELF: Take pleasure in doing more than you thought you could, even if you're not there yet.

Patience counters the frustration of going slower than you'd like. Ben Franklin said, "He that can have patience can have what he will." You might not be ready. Patience to take baby steps strengthens your chance to stay on top. Robin learned:

I felt frustrated by my lack of progress. It was never enough. Anger at what I hadn't done yet clouded appreciation for what I did. When I got help from a previously one-way friend, I told my sister I couldn't believe it. She asked why, since everyone noticed me speaking up more. Everyone but me! After that I cheered each step. That made me want to improve my behavior even more. Now I'm bursting with pride!

Do you want instant gratification? Change takes time. You may feel frustrated and impatient and give up. After all, a Twinkie tastes better than the scale dropping half a pound a week. But that's twenty-six pounds a year! Baby steps add up. During setbacks, accept that you're human, don't get angry, and try again. Enjoy recapturing control. You've had a lifetime to get here and the rest of your life to get where you're going. Whitney says:

I used to see only the big picture. The concept of acknowledging little steps seemed silly, but I tried. When I set a small boundary with Mom, she didn't get it. Normally I'd have seen that as failure but instead said, "Congratulations for trying" in the mirror— better than feeling like a loser! It took several follow-throughs for Mom to bend. Unbelievable! If I hadn't praised myself for each attempt, I'd have given up. Now she respects me more, and I'm setting boundaries for people I never thought would change. But they didn't change. I did!

EXERCISE: Write down each new response to someone after you make it, however small and even if you don't get the results you want. Watch them add up to more satisfaction as your actions stick!

When I consciously took each step, I was terrified and then exhilarated as I got small results. If one didn't work, I tried again. Eventually new habits stick when you get stronger and your new attitude replaces old habits more often. Each step increases empowerment. Even stopping a habit sometimes is a power move. With setbacks, how you handle them determines whether you progress or quit. Fight excuses to postpone action and prompt yourself to continue to take control. Pay attention to your behavior and tweak it to cue people differently. Self-awareness is the power tool of change. You can't appreciate or change what you don't recognize. Nasrin learned:

I could say no for the first time when I recognized my value as an individual and understood that I deserve the best. In fact, self-awareness was my best motivation to take care of myself and not settle for unsatisfactory situations, behavior, etc. Self-awareness is the biggest start. I've already observed miracles through it.

 NOTE TO SELF: Repetition strengthens good habits and makes them automatic.

Role Models

Hone your people-watching skills. You don't have to ask someone to be a role model, though that's good too. Observe someone you admire to discover techniques for more effective behavior. Emulate what might work for you that can guide you to new ways. What tone of voice or words does she use? How does she handle specific situations or respond to difficult people? Sonia told a support group about an executive she admired. We encouraged studying her behavior. The next week she was excited:

This exec has everyone's respect. No one gossips about her, and she gets support. I paid attention and observed specific aspects of her behavior and personality for a week to discern how she spoke to others that I could try. For example, she smiles before speaking to put people at ease and keeps her voice steady under pressure. I'm slowly emulating her. As I practice, there's a change already.

Study many people. Note specific things you like and why. You may observe a certain method of communication, a way of walking, a technique for handling anger, etc. I still look for qualities to incorporate into my persona. Create new habits by discovering better ones! Jodee made it work:

> *When you grow up in a family having difficulty with alcohol, drugs, disease, etc., the children are forced to look to alternative persons or activities in building a composite for their adult life. I chose pieces of a number of people—teachers, friends' parents, employers—until the pieces I respected and liked were merged with my own to develop my own style.*

✌ Letting In the Light ✌

. . . .

"Any change, even a change for the better, is always accompanied by drawbacks and discomforts."

—Arnold Bennett

If you want to be a Nice Girl on Top, pay more attention to *you*. What's holding you back? Therapy can help guide you past blocks. When you learn to handle the basics, your empowerment increases. Michelle found support in therapy:

> *Therapy taught me how important my feelings and emotions are to my general health and also to the people around me. I saw an alternative therapist who believes that our physical problems are a manifestation of our thoughts and feelings. We began with my physical issues and traced them back to the emotional blockages they stemmed from. I'm still in the process of clearing and reevaluating, but working with a therapist to resolve issues from my past taught me to approach problems very differently.*

Conscious Self-Appreciation

It's harder to notice your wonderful qualities if you focus on flaws. What you dislike can blind you to your good details. Someone dragged me to a mirror so I could appreciate my pretty green eyes. All I saw was cellulite and unruly hair, which I hated. A personal inventory creates consciousness. Self-esteem isn't about looks! It's who you are. Recognizing your positives builds confidence and radiates to make you more attractive! Michelle says:

> *Spending time understanding exactly who I am and why I am unique helped me appreciate myself a lot more. Most of all, I'm proud of the energy and positivity I have, and I've decided to surround myself with the same type of people.*

EXERCISE: List what you recognize as good qualities and also what others like about you. Ask friends for suggestions. Don't just list the obvious. What do you do well or get compliments for? Nice handwriting? A good sense of humor? Clever skills?

Read your list often to consciously value your assets. Over time, with awareness of your worthy attributes, you *can* learn to truly like yourself. Develop qualities in yourself that you like in others. Do you enjoy being with DoorMats? If so, continue being one! You'll attract other DoorMats and those who use them. If you like people with their acts together, do your best to straighten yours. What qualities in others draw you? How can you develop them? Consciously cultivate the simpler traits first. Self-appreciation makes it easier to love yourself. Practice being kinder to you! It's a delightful exercise once you accept that you deserve it. Heidi recommends:

It's great to ask for things you need and want, but feed yourself first. Give yourself everything you need; let the universe give you everything you need. And then there isn't really much that you have to ask for.

EXERCISE: Create awareness lists. Write down as many details as possible.

- Values in Others That I'd Like in Myself
- Personality Traits I'd Love to Have
- Things I Especially Appreciate in a Friend
- How I Want the World to See Me
- How I Want to See Me

As you try to fulfill your needs and what brings you pleasure, self-love increases, as tolerance for unacceptable behavior decreases. Self-love feels better than criticism! Say "I love you" in the mirror. The more loving you are, the more you'll enjoy it. Self-love nurtures your power. Yassmin found it:

Appreciating myself comes from my ability to integrate socially, get along with people from different backgrounds, be in a foreign country and feel at home. I'm proud of starting from zero and building my life to discover the ultimate truth—that being happy is easy and simple when you love yourself. I do my best to please others, but I'm sometimes the last thing they think about. That's a good reason to develop some self-loving!

Minding Your Head

If you doubt you can do something, you probably won't. Change begins in your head. You choose to let what happened in the past affect you today. Remaining a People Pleaser is your choice. *You* have the power to stop negative thoughts and beliefs about you. If you think them, they control you. No one can tell you what to think, only what you could think. It's your choice to listen. Your power starts with remembering:

▶ No one can get into your head unless you allow it.
▶ Stereotypes can't stick if you dismiss them.
▶ The past can't hurt unless you embrace old beliefs.
▶ What someone says about you isn't true unless you accept it as truth.

NOTE TO SELF: You get the respect you expect.

Whose perception rules you? Mom's? The media's? Your romantic partner's? We give too much importance to what others think. A Nice Girl on Top creates her own perception. How you see yourself and project it commands respect or footprints. Watch for your own distorted perceptions, such as:

▶ That extra five pounds make you fat.
▶ The five-minute incident ruins your day.
▶ One mistake makes you a screwup.
▶ One boyfriend who's a jerk means you're a poor judge of men.
▶ You don't know something, so you're stupid.

Enough already! Girlfriend, don't be your own worst enemy by blowing flaws or problems out of proportion. I remember seeing only what I hated in the mirror—never my pretty face. For years I was fat and ugly. Looking back, I was far from that. But a few extra pounds drastically altered my perception. When I accepted my body as soft, curvy, and sexy, I got more attractive and thinner without losing weight! Perception is *your* choice. Do you distort yours as excuses for not taking risks?

- ▶ "I've never gotten respect. I'm no good!" The past is history. *Now* is what counts. It doesn't matter how people treated you before. You know better.
- ▶ "I can never finish anything." Just because you haven't finished things, you're not hopeless. Take baby steps to complete a project and prove that you can!
- ▶ "I should be further along in my career, so I'm a loser." Says who? Individuals work on different timelines. Not advancing enough doesn't make you a loser unless you choose to be. Learn more skills!
- ▶ "People don't like me." Paranoia will destroy ya. Do you expect rejection and pull back? Act friendly and expect friendliness.

If you expect to achieve goals, you will—if you don't give up. It may take longer than you'd like, but you'll get there. Other people's beliefs don't matter. Only your view counts. If you're told "You're stupid," you can think "I won't get far being stupid" or "I know I'm smart." Do you assume inability before trying?

- ▶ "I'm fat." This wounds self-esteem. Instead, say "I love and accept myself as I am." "I'm not fat, I'm curvy."
- ▶ "I was never good at math and can't do budgets." Leave problems in school at school! Instead, think "I'll try my best to learn."
- ▶ "I'm a klutz, so how can I join a gym?" *Klutz, slow, shy,* etc., are self-imposed bars in the prison of limitations. Let go of excuses that keep you from trying things. Often klutzes are klutzes because they expect to be.

NOTE TO SELF: If you repeat beliefs, they expand as truth. "That was clumsy" becomes "I'm clumsy," which grows into "I'm limited in what I can do because I'm clumsy." Roadblock alert!

"Woe is me" and "I'll never get there" become negative affirmations. Defy them by framing yourself more positively and not in extremes. You make a mistake and think "I always screw up." Limit mistakes to the moment. "I made a mistake but do lots right." If negatives invade your thoughts, use positive affirmations! One of my favorites is "Stop! No more negatives! This is the first minute of the rest of my life, and I *choose* only positives." Or "I won't accept this anymore." Melania said in class:

My unsupportive parents said I wasn't good for much. I'd never get a good job or man. My friend shot that down with compliments when I whined, which felt good. I realized my life sucked since I expected it to and decided to change. While I didn't believe it, I affirmed, "I'm worthy of a good job (or man)." I repeated them when nasty thoughts came. With practice, I'm starting to believe them. I have a better job and am meeting kinder men. There's more to do, but I'm choosing a positive direction and like feeling in control—and happier. All by changing my thoughts!

If you feel inadequate, consciously tackle situations more positively. I had a bad experience at a gym and for years believed "I can't lift weights." Then I started slowly with a trainer. Each session instilled more confidence. I learned form and got revved when people noticed. Now I confidently work out and actually get respect from muscle guys. You can baby-step to your desire by changing beliefs. Courtney says:

My kindergarten teacher made fun of my paintings. At five, I was convinced I had no artistic ability. The funny thing was I loved art and made pictures but hid them. When I took a handicrafts workshop, I laughed when my teacher praised me and asked me to teach a class since I was so good. I babbled that my kindergarten teacher had determined I had no talent. She insisted I did. I began showing my art to friends, exhibited at a local fair, and sold some. Now I consider myself an artist. The only change was my thoughts.

EXERCISE: Ask yourself, "How do I limit myself or get in my way?"

Too often we hurt ourselves for not being perfect. Yes, things go wrong. That's life. Even with my strong faith, there are setbacks. I allow downtime and then work to bring my mind back in synch with my beliefs. It's not easy, but you can do it! Talk to yourself in loving ways. It's your choice to focus on what's right with you or obsess about what's wrong. Change your world with positive thoughts!

Redefining Modesty

Modesty—being low-key about achievements—is drummed into girls. Were you taught that it's not nice to speak well of yourself much? This isn't taught to guys. Were you taught to downplay your strong points so people will like you? Women often shrug off accomplishments and own failure. Stop!

▶ "I must be lucky" should be "Damn, I'm good!"
▶ "Everyone did well" should be "I'm proud that I led the team well."

Yet if something goes wrong, you take responsibility:

▶ "I should have known the client would change his mind" should be "I'm not a mind reader. Things just happen."
▶ "I let Mom down again" should be "Mom expects too much. I can only try my best."

How do you perceive achievements? Are you proud, or do you downplay or give others credit? I'd extol someone else's contribution and respond to compliments by belittling myself—until I became a Nice Girl on Top. Take that first step—say thanks to a compliment and shut your mouth! Modesty reinforces self-doubt. Express pride. If a friend resents it, reconsider her friendship. Tanika chucked modesty:

My mother said it wasn't ladylike to talk about myself. So I'd minimize everything and shoot down compliments. It became so automatic that I stopped noticing things to be proud of. When my new assistant said she hoped to be like me someday, I laughed, warning her to wait till she got to know me better. Lena said she understood. Her mother said many women don't feel pride, but that's rubbish. Lena continued praising me, and slowly I swapped modesty for pride.

EXERCISE: Think of an accomplishment or good deed you did recently. Tell someone about it without downplaying it. Start in the mirror if necessary. Then share with Mom and then others. Practicing expressing joy in what you do!

Break the habit of diluting achievements with distorted modesty! A confident woman is proud of her successes and shares them with passion. Pride in your achievements makes you interesting. Next time you do something special, or make even a small accomplishment, give yourself a thumbs-up in a mirror. Scream with joy and say "Damn, I'm good" or "I'm proud of me!" Get excited. Praising yourself helps you accept it from others and boosts your self-image.

7

Declaring Your Personal Independence

"When you change the way you look at things,
the things you look at change."

—WAYNE DYER

WOULD YOU LIKE to implement the power you already possess? Yes, you already possess it! It just needs activation. Declare independence—from other people's needs, from insecurity, from friends who use you, from disrespectful people, from not being taken seriously, and from letting others determine your direction. When you light your fire inside, it radiates throughout you. Learn to satisfy your needs so what others do is gravy. Nice Girls on Top learn how to get things done if there's no assistance and go out solo if no one can join them. We have a lot more fun!

⌇ Making Friends with You ⌇

"*The talent for being happy is appreciating and liking what you have, instead of what you don't have.*"

—WOODY ALLEN

How WOULD YOU feel if a friend called you fat for having ice cream? It would ruin your pleasure. What if she called you stupid for making a mistake? You'd feel angry and hurt and think she should be kinder. You wouldn't do that to her. Yet you'd do it to yourself. Be your own friend by acting like one! Nice Girls on Top know their best friend is the one in the mirror. Nasrin agrees:

> After experiencing many ups and downs, I know that the only person who can help me change my life for the better is me. Others may guide me, but the first step has to be mine. I will lose many people, including dear ones, during my life, but I'm always with myself until the last breath. I can never leave me alone. It's up to me to criticize myself all the time in a destructive way or to treat myself as a friend.

Seeking perfection makes you overly self-critical. That's not loving! Yet you'd never be so unkind and unsupportive to another friend. Why are you different?

Nurturing from the Inside Out

Everyone needs me time: when *you* choose what *you* want for *you*. Fear of being alone kept me a DoorMat. I'd treat for dinner or a movie to have company. Now I see solo time as *my* way! Mala says, "It's a chance to enjoy the quiet and listen to my own thoughts. Very often I use this time to mentally check in with myself to make sure I'm feeling good about things." Fear of being alone drives you to kiss up to others. So redefine *alone*! Your own company can feel good if you let it. Yassmin agrees:

> I enjoy time alone. I can learn a lot more than with others, shut my phone and door, and live with my movies, books, music, and thoughts. No one can interrupt my train of thought. I get annoyed

when I hear my roommate talking for hours on the phone without saying anything interesting. I've always done things for fun alone, like movies, concerts, museums.

NOTE TO SELF: You can be lonely even with someone.

Find interests you enjoy and nurture them. Go out with just you—when and how you want. Find fun friends! Develop hobbies. It's lovely to make decisions (what movie, where to eat, etc.) based solely on your desires. I'm thrilled with time to read, write, or just do silly things. Jodee says, "A benefit of solo is being able to think creatively without being pulled in multiple directions." Empower yourself by getting a life so fear of loneliness won't drive you to remain a People Pleaser. Michelle says:

I know that relaxing and watching a movie or treating myself to dinner if I've had a bad day is just as important as the washing that hasn't been done or the dust behind the refrigerator. All that stuff will still be there tomorrow.

EXERCISE: List at least five things you've wanted to try and figure out a way to try at least one.

When you're happy inside and enjoy your company, you win, no matter whom you cut loose. It eases fear of taking a stand. Ask yourself, "What would make me happy?" If it's within reason, do it! Splurge on a massage or treat occasionally. Women say they're hesitant to spend money, yet many spend on others, especially guys. Hello! You count more! No matter how busy you are, grant yourself permission for downtime. Relaxation, fun activities, or time with friends is healthy. Balance obligations with fun, as Jen does:

> *I have plenty of hobbies and a daunting workload, but I keep my life in perspective. I can blow off work to play golf on a warm day once in a while, as long as my work responsibilities are taken care of. I'd buy a huge TV with my credit card as long as I can allocate funds. We live in a society where we expect immediate gratification. You can't always give in to tempting impulses. It's important to consider consequences of your actions but give yourself some treats. There are always things we don't want to do. The sooner I get those over with, the sooner I do the fun things.*

Be self-loving by cutting your best friend—*you*—slack. Sometimes you might not work as fast as hoped. It's OK! Try your best. Shortcomings don't make you bad or a loser. At parties, my willpower goes on hiatus. I pig out—guilt free—and take control after. When I'd reassure a friend who beat herself up during occasional pig-outs that one indulgence wouldn't ruin her, she punished herself with each bite, chanting, "I'm a bad girl." I doubt she enjoyed anything. Take pleasure, not guilt trips, in splurging!

EXERCISE: Plan a "me" day. Figure out what you want to do during a whole day that's all about you. Go where you want and when. Write it in your datebook, as a date with you!

Counting Your Blessings

Some women unhappily lament what they don't have. Stoking your appreciation for life's blessings—big and small—elicits a better mood. Don't take small blessings for granted, Naomi explains:

My husband, my parents, my sister, and all of us having our health is what I count among my blessings. If we are blessed with health and then enjoy happiness, success, and wealth in our chosen professions, that is luck and the fruits of hard work, which we never would have experienced without the blessing of health.

A spiritual mind-set makes it easier to feel supported when taking a stand. Without my strong faith, I'd still be a whining People Pleaser! Use faith for strength in your rise to the top of your life. Michelle says:

Faith helped me see the bigger picture and stop worrying about little things. I firmly believe that everything happens for a reason, and I already have all that I currently deserve and am ready for. With this belief comes a great sense of power, comfort, and purpose.

Focus on positives by counting your blessings. Estelle says, "I believe that living in a state of gratitude and believing in God's abundance brings prosperity into my life." It sure works for me! Mala agrees that consciousness of blessings brings more:

By counting my blessings I receive even more to be thankful for. It used to be very important that everyone like me. That is, until I realized by trying to please everyone else I often neglected my own feelings. I count my blessings for my true friends and loved ones. I don't need to neglect my own needs to make them happy. Now I attract friendships that are grounded in mutual acceptance.

EXERCISE: List every little thing you're grateful for. Appreciate things like sunshine, a friendly doorman, your freedom, healthy family, good eyesight, etc. List *anything* that gives you pleasure, satisfaction, relief from problems, etc.

Become aware of small blessings you take for granted. Next time you feel "Woe is me," count your blessings to remember the good in your life. We all have some! Amy says:

> *I consider blessings all that I am thankful for. One thing I try to do as often as I can is "gratitude lists"—a cool idea a good friend passed on. Whenever I am able, whether I feel great or not, I take time to sit down, focus, and write a list of things for which I am grateful and happy to have in my life. A few phrases and—no matter what—my mood improves. I am calmer and filled with greater joy—a powerful mental shift and a positive frequency to be aware of! The trick is perspective. The best thing is, I e-mail these quick lists to a handful of select friends. I am on several others' gratitude lists as well. Every time you receive one, it is a drop of sunshine in your day and inspires you to be more grateful in turn. I have even inspired my sister to write her own lists; others too. We are all blessed with gifts and grace, and the more we recognize and* acknowledge *this practice-shifting viewpoint, the more peace radiates in our lives.*

Even if life takes a bad turn, faith allows you to accept that there's a reason for what you didn't want—the difference between being a victim of circumstances and overcoming them. The more you consciously appreciate blessings, the more happiness—the real kind! Expect more blessings. I get them often. You can too!

✍ A Stronger Kind of Nice ✍

....

"Not being able to govern events, I govern myself."
—MICHEL DE MONTAIGNE

If you want a better life, take charge! The stronger you become, the more you'll act accordingly. When you give yourself friendship and value who you are, you own your life!

Taking the Wheel

A great way to feel more in control is to work on counterproductive habits. List what you don't like and slowly change those habits. A boyfriend made fun of my cluttered closets. I got defensive but realized I hated having things piled on shelves like a flea market! After ditching him, I took control by sorting clutter into pretty shopping bags and shoe boxes. Having them neatly lined on my shelves made me feel astoundingly better about me. Controlling habits is a huge self-esteem booster! Work on what you apologize for, like me with my clutter.

 NOTE TO SELF: Cleaning is a fantastic way to take control.

When I feel down or unfocused, I organize and get rid of stuff. Clutter busting gives you control and makes room for better things. Begin with one room. I chose my bathroom and slowly made a habit of wiping things down each day. Seeing it sparkle gives me pride. The kitchen was next. My place isn't always neat, but my kitchen and bathroom are. I take control regularly instead of deferring to my inner slob. Judith says:

> *I always tossed stuff down at home and made excuses for the mess to visitors. When I cleared my hall table, I felt pride. As I got neater, my self-image improved dramatically. It gave me some control. One at a time I'm breaking habits. I feel so much control in general just from the first step—clearing a table!*

Bad habits reinforce feeling out of control. Each time you're criticized for lighting a cigarette, self-esteem lowers. Every pound gained diminishes power. You can take charge of negative habits. Don't think in terms of dieting, quitting smoking, ending tardiness, becoming neat, etc. You're taking control of habits:

▶ *If you smoke,* try for one less cigarette a day for a week. Write the number on your calendar each day. If you slip, try again tomorrow. As you adapt to one less smoke, eliminate one more. Even if you don't stop, you're taking control.

▶ *No more diets!* Affirm, "I can control my eating." What would you normally eat? Eliminate something. Have an open-face sandwich or use vinaigrette instead of a creamy dressing on your salad. Going out for dinner? It's not all or nothing. Have one roll instead of two. If dessert matters, skip something to compensate. Exercise because it feels good.

▶ *Clear stuff.* Hang bags on doorknobs around your living space. Pop what you can live without into a bag. I use white for throwaways; colored for giveaways. It slowly controls clutter. The bags make me more conscious of making room!

▶ *Always late?* Don't vow to always be on time. Try for one day. What makes you late? Not allowing enough time? Distractions? Pick one day to be on time for something. Leave earlier. Arriving on time gives you control of that moment! Try another day and slowly break habits that make you late.

EXERCISE: Take control using my fifteen-minute rule. Don't fight cravings—for a cigarette, drink, sweet, getting lost on the Internet instead of working, etc. Postpone the craving for fifteen minutes. Consciously congratulate yourself for some control. Then try to wait another fifteen. You may eventually have it but will feel more control. Cravings subside as empowerment increases.

Stay focused on each step that works instead of being discouraged by goofs. Tackle one habit at a time. Progress achieved slowly is more likely to stick. Try martial arts—a great discipline for learning control and techniques that build confidence. The more control, the more confidence replaces insecurity. Lindsay says:

> *I never felt confident. When you said to improve one thing, I chose PowerPoint. I stopped stressing about other things, practiced, and got guidance. I became good, and faster, which allows me more time to conquer other tasks. The more I did, the more my control over other things. Now I'm seeking a better job with my new skills and confidence.*

I Choose to Be Happy!

Many of us live in a state of waiting for the right time to be happy. Dependence on outside factors or validation from others keeps happiness beyond our control. Real happiness is an inside job! The right moment for joy is *now*! Reaching goals first is counterproductive. "When I meet the 'right' guy, I'll be happy." Why wait to find someone for what you can give yourself? Jen says:

> *It's not someone else's role to make you happy. You can be happy with a person, he can add to your happiness, she can cheer you up, but if you are unhappy about yourself or your life, you need to figure out why and take steps to change this. I'm talking about internal happiness. People look for happiness outside themselves: "if I get plastic surgery or that new BMW, if I move into that gated community, etc., I will be happy." You can buy moments of happiness and fulfillment. But outside happiness comes and goes in waves. You'll want plastic surgery again, there will be a new BMW, and when a friend moves into the bigger gated community, you might find yourself unhappy and unfulfilled with your life. Internal happiness keeps us in balance.*

NOTE TO SELF: Happiness is a choice. Choose to be happy *now*.

Don't postpone happiness until you lose "enough" weight, get married, have "enough" money, or reach some other milestone. I may not have everything I'd like, but I'm happy! If it's raining when I wake, I choose to smile and count my blessings. I've heard, "I'll work on my self-esteem after losing weight." Good self-esteem means accepting yourself *now*, as is. Don't postpone pleasure. "I won't get married until I'm a size eight." "I'll buy new clothes after I lose ten pounds." That's penance—"I'm bad for not being thinner, so I deny myself what I'd like." Not feeling worthy of happiness until you improve deprives you. You deserve what you'd like *now*. Yassmin says:

> *My favorite quote, by Storm Jameson, says, "Happiness comes from the capacity to feel freely, to enjoy simply, to think deeply, to risk life, to be needed." That's how I see happiness and try to think forward, positively. I push away bad thoughts and most of all have goals, therefore finding meaning in my life.*

Waiting for self-improvement to be happy is self-inflicted punishment for feeling imperfect. Years ago I lived in a far from ideal house. I wanted nice things but was advised to wait until I moved. My roommates roughed it on room decor. I got curtains, pretty pictures, and frills. They teased me, not understanding why I fussed over my inferior living space. My bedroom made me feel at home, comfy and content, while they were grouchy. When I moved, my treasures joined me. Creating a wonderful home environment is an act of love. Forgive imperfections or past failures. Slowly give yourself permission to be happy *now*. Robin says:

My mother withheld treats until I got good grades or lost weight. Feeling inadequate made me self-critical. It's hard to be happy when you hate yourself. I always wanted to go to Paris, but not until I lost fifty pounds. I lived in wishful thinking—if I was only this or that, I'd be happy. As my confidence grew and I began to love me right now, slowly I stopped looking outside. I love being a good person. And I'm leaving for Paris! It will make me happier, since I'm already happy.

EXERCISE: List why you deserve to be happy. If you're short on reasons, ask friends for help.

People Pleasers compromise happiness by making decisions based on what they think others want them to do. A Nice Girl on Top chooses what she wants. Pursue your own path with a vengeance and enjoy the ride. Parents reward kids for achievements. Adults can reward themselves just because. . . . Why put off for the "right" time what you can enjoy now? Think about why you postpone. You don't become more worthier because you lose weight or reach a milestone.

Make happiness your goal every day. I'd like to lose weight but am happy to buy my current body nice clothes *now*! And while I'd love to be deliciously wrapped in a man who rocks my world, I'm happy rocking my own. A great guy won't make me happy. He'd make me happier. I'm already happy. Jen says:

I'm happy with my self-image and accomplishments. I have goals and do my best to reach them. I am confident. This is true happiness to me. It's something that can't be bought per se, but it is something that can be felt. People feel the energy, the enthusiasm from internally happy people. They are people that other people want to be around—as if their outlook on life and lifestyle will instantaneously transfer over to others by association.

Do you want to be perfect or to be happy? Decide whether striving for perfection is worth the price of sacrificing joy. Living for the future hurts your present. Why postpone gratification by waiting for the right circumstances? To me, the biggest success is being happy. Take a step in that direction *now!*

♫ Winning Over Fear ♫

"You gain strength, courage, and confidence by every experience in which you really stop and look fear in the face. . . . You must do the things you think you cannot do."

—ELEANOR ROOSEVELT

FEAR BLOCKS YOU from expressing feelings, asking for a promotion, letting people go, saying no to requests, and many other things. Everyone experiences it. It can be subconscious or subtle. Nowadays reality shows encourage fighting fear. People survive eating pig's innards and bugs. They perform death-defying feats and survive on deserted islands. If they can get beyond it, so can you! François de La Rochefoucauld said, "We promise according to our hopes and perform according to our fears." Think about decisions you've made based on fear. You can conquer worries, one baby step at a time, *if* you choose to.

Fraidy Girls

Are you afraid of what might happen if you take a stand? Jumping out of a plane causes legitimate frazzled nerves. But often we're scared of the unknown—"what-ifs" instead of concrete situations. Imagination can conjure up potential worst-case scenarios. What if she hates me if I can't babysit? Or I'm fired for not working weekends? Irrational speculations can freeze you. On a TV talk show, Roseanne said:

> *My next-door neighbor wanted to move my fence, and I told her not to. She did it anyway. I was very upset, but what could I do? She won't sell her house, and I won't sell mine. Since we're staying neighbors, I must keep peace. I'm afraid to start with her, so I let her get away with it. I wish I wasn't a DoorMat, but I'm afraid.*

 NOTE TO SELF: The unknown is usually worse than what really happens!

I asked what she was afraid of. "The neighbor has a dog." It sounded irrational, as fear often is. Roseanne was sheepish. She'd built fear of confronting her neighbor around a dog, yet when asked, she had no idea how it could hurt her. Unknown outcomes are scary. If you request a promotion that's denied, you may need another job. If you tell your boyfriend you won't accept poor behavior, it may mean breaking up. Sienna warns that fear pervades your whole life if you don't control it:

> *When I complained about being dumped on at work, friends asked why I took it. I was afraid! And felt low. My boyfriend used me. My mechanic overcharged me. I was scared to argue. My dad insisted the fear thing must stop. He was right! I'd become miserable. It was silly not to contest being overcharged. So I did. The outcome? A refund! I asked my manager to clarify my duties at work. He was surprised but reassigned some tasks. I told my boyfriend to shape*

*up or bye. The jury is still out on him, but I'll live if we break up.
I'm happier in control!*

When fear creates a belief that you need someone or what someone has to offer, you lose control. There are other jobs, boyfriends, and friends. Step back from fear to see your choices objectively. Don't let fear create self-fulfilling prophecies. If you believe you can't live without someone's approval, help, or love, you make them too important. Fear magnifies problems and needs. Crumbs taste sweet when you're scared of getting nothing. Leaving or expressing yourself tastes sweeter.

Making Friends with Fear

Mark Twain said, "Courage is resistance to fear, mastery of fear—not absence of fear." Courageous people progress despite being scared. Courage allows you to get past it and learn there's less to worry about than you thought. Overcome fear by doing what you're afraid of. When you handle it, confidence builds. You'll be scared again, but next time will be a smidgen easier. Fight what scares you by taking action! Facing fear teaches you that you can manage most situations.

> **EXERCISE:** Are you nervous about messing up? Does fear stop you from expressing dissatisfaction or setting ground rules? Write down what scares you. Read each one aloud, declare, "This won't stop me!" and burn it.

How likely is your worst-case scenario to actually happen? Analyze the layers and diffuse them by assessing what really scares you and recognizing that it's not as bad as you've made it out to be. Ask what's the worst that can happen. Then decide: can I cope with it? Be honest. You don't have to like the outcome, but can you handle it? I did a Fire Walk and learned there are always choices. Identifying exactly what scares you puts fear into perspective. Facing fiery hot coals was scary. But I recognized that if it burned too much I'd jump off. It would be embarrassing, but I'd cope. Then I walked the length of coals. It was empowering to beat fear. Sophia learned in my workshop:

> *I missed a lot in my scaredy-Soph days. I never tried advancing at work. I was terrified of screwing up and needed to be liked. When I realized fear was a projection and not reality, I examined it. The worst that could happen? I'd lose a friend who used me? My boss would know I expected respect? I took more risks once I recognized the fear in my head was worse than the likely results. Even if things don't go well, I'm OK.*

What's the worst that could happen? Will you starve if you speak up and get fired? Will life end if your man books? Mara says, "I still get nervous, but you have to just do it. Make the calls even though you're nervous about it." When you identify exactly what may happen, find ways to cope. If fear controls your decisions:

▶ Acknowledge out loud that you're scared.
▶ Identify exactly what scares you.
▶ Ask yourself how you can move past a negative result and not let it control your life.
▶ Think about the best outcomes, not the worst.
▶ Expect the best.
▶ Do something; don't let fear paralyze you.

NOTE TO SELF: "The only thing we have to fear is fear itself." (Franklin Delano Roosevelt)

Feeling scared is normal. Facing fear empowers you. It's your choice to succumb or to conquer it. Put out feelers for other jobs. Plan fun things in case you cut ties with someone. Be proud of yourself for doing what scared you. Take baby steps away from fears. Stop imagining what might happen and focus on what's happening now. Right *now* you're OK. There will always be obstacles and people who aren't cooperative. That's reality! But you can hold on to self-control. Try Mala's tip:

> *Whenever I have to face a challenge, I give myself pep talks. I tell myself it's going to be OK. Even as I'm confronting my fear, inside I talk to myself as my own best friend and cheerleader. I tell myself things like "You're doing great. It's OK. You can do this!"*

You *can* do this if you tell yourself you can!

8

"What Part of *No* Don't You Understand?"

"It is not the mountain we conquer, but ourselves."

—SIR EDMUND HILLARY

ᴘᴇᴏᴘʟᴇ Pʟᴇᴀsᴇʀs ᴋᴇᴇᴘ their mouths shut to seem agreeable. Do you worry about alienating people by speaking up? Nice Girls on Top know that real friends will celebrate your growth and accept that *no* is *not* a dirty word!

⌇ Turning Over Your Welcome Mat ⌇

"Be who you are and say what you feel, because those who mind don't matter and those who matter don't mind."

—Dʀ. Seuss

Exᴘʀᴇssɪɴɢ ʏᴏᴜʀsᴇʟꜰ ɪs liberating. If you're hesitant, imagine the consequences of holding feelings in and the regret that will follow. Then speak up—nicely, with an approach that shows you're serious.

Getting Comfortable with Speaking Up

Express yourself in small doses instead of socking it to people. For example, if Mom always nags that you do nothing right, calmly explain why her claim bothers you and change the subject so she can process what you've said. Don't dump everything. Reinforce points periodically until they get through. If you lose someone, it may be for the best, as Tara discovered:

> *I loved finding a friend when I moved to a large city. But Marie was often nasty and controlling. I complained to everyone but Marie, afraid to lose a friend to do activities with. She did awful things and then became temporarily sweet, but I wanted her company. As my self-esteem increased, I gently told Marie that she and the anger drained me. She disappeared. I began doing activities Marie didn't like and met nicer friends. Wish I'd spoken sooner.*

 NOTE TO SELF: If you don't speak up clearly, how can people know what you want?

Be straightforward, with concrete examples and suggestions. "I don't like that" gets little resolution. Explain why and what you'd appreciate. Don't drop hints and pray they stick. Give details. Derek warns:

> *Ladies, speak up! Nobody can read your mind. I told my wife she could join me at a conference. Kelly immediately said she shouldn't go but sulked until I left. When I returned, she was upset. She had wanted to go yet insisted it was a bad idea! At work women dance around issues instead of being straight. One says what's on her mind without getting emotional and earns respect! Instead of complaining to friends, be straightforward.*

Do you ignore unfair sniping? Critical people do target practice, under the guise of "trying to help." You may be advised to lose
weight or act the "right way." It can hurt but continues if you're
silent. Calmly set dart throwers straight. Yelling shows they scored.
Explain those comments will no longer be tolerated. Staying cool
is empowering. If emotions rise, step back, take deep breaths, and
repeat, "I can control criticism." Then *you*, not the one pushing
your buttons, have control. Mala finds it easiest to communicate as
soon as she becomes aware of what she needs:

> In the past, I'd wait for the person to notice the problem. After a
> long while I'd become resentful. By the time I'd summon the cour-
> age to ask for what I wanted I'd be angry. I realized I was making
> the situation much more difficult than it needed to be. So now I
> go to the person and preface it by saying "This isn't easy for me to
> say, but it's bothering me, so I need to tell you." My motivation, in
> this case, is trying to short-circuit my anger before it gets out of
> control.

EXERCISE: Practice several comeback statements to make when
people say inappropriate things so you're prepared instead of
flustered when it happens. Be sure to say them with a smile!

Staring Down Intimidation

Manipulators catch you off guard with accusations, demands, and
unwarranted guilt. You can smell word manure if you pay attention. Getting angry may egg them on. A big smile confuses them.
I often laugh to show how ridiculous their words are. Intimidators
hate that. They want *you* to be uncomfortable. Why not beat them
at their own game! Jessie stood up to her cousin:

Willie is lazy and rarely helps his mom. Since I love my aunt, I take her to do errands. But I do that for my mom too. I told Willie to take over. He cajoled me with how much more she likes me there and called me selfish, like I'm responsible for his mom. In the past I backed down. Now I told him to face a mirror when he says "selfish." He can't back me into a corner anymore and needs to step up. I'll do what I can on my terms!

NOTE TO SELF: You're *entitled* to set boundaries for what you do for others.

Fake confidence and handle intimidators sweetly. If you're yelled at, force your mouth shut to annoy them by not reacting. Just nod and say "Uh-huh." That's staying in control, which controls the situation. Intimidators may seem scary but usually aren't. Eileen proved this when a mechanic tried to hold her car hostage. She explains:

My fan belt snapped. But Marty said I needed an oil change and there were dangerously worn parts. I just wanted to drive my car home. He acted like, without work, my car would die. I knew he was trying to take advantage and calmly asked him to change the belt so I could leave. He insisted on more repairs. I calmly called a friend on my cell and asked her to call the attorney general's office to report an unethical mechanic. Marty immediately fixed the belt. My mechanic confirmed that Marty's claim was bogus!

State only what's necessary. The nicer you are as you confront intimidation, the more you'll rankle them. If they don't stop, quietly challenge back with a smile. Make the person defensive instead:

- ▶ "Why am I wrong to turn you down when you do it often?"
- ▶ "Why call it a loan when it's never repaid? I can't afford more."
- ▶ "I'm curious. Why do you think you're more important than me?"
- ▶ "Why is it helpful to hurt my feelings?"

Etc.! Look the intimidator straight in the eyes and smile as you speak. A sweet approach feels better than ranting and defending yourself. People won't know what to make of assertive words spoken so nicely. Sami called after a workshop:

> *I often succumbed when people put me on the defensive but am turning the tables. Mom insinuated I wasn't a good daughter if I didn't jump for her. I asked what she considered a good mother since she scoffed at my needs. Mom got insulted. I was prepared with examples—pushing me to break dates, missing opportunities and other things to prove I was a good daughter. She got defensive but couldn't reply. I explained I need boundaries, and she's actually trying. Now I'm challenging other intimidators!*

 NOTE TO SELF: You don't have to accept fallout from someone's rage.

Verbal abuse leaves no physical scars but cuts you. Consistently being berated hurts. Continuous apologies feel demeaning. Been there; done that! I endured undeserved anger to avoid losing the person. Have you excused it after someone:

- ▶ apologized after calming down?
- ▶ insisted it's your fault?

- ▶ brought you flowers?
- ▶ labeled you too sensitive?
- ▶ justified behavior as kidding around?

None of this makes verbal abuse right! Don't suffer silently. Nice Girls on Top recognize meanness as abuse. Everyone has an occasional bad day. But someone's regularly taking frustration or anger out on you is unacceptable. Speak up!

Nice Girls on Top Get Heard!

Were you taught it's ladylike to be seen but not heard? Keeping quiet is *not* ladylike. It's DoorMatlike. In the old days, ladies kept quiet. No more! Talking around issues achieves little. You can communicate without alienating people. Even if you disagree or challenge them, do it nicely. But don't go overboard trying to make a point, as Michelle says:

> *I'm learning to talk less and say more. I make a conscious effort to listen to what people say, notice what they imply, and then cater to that. I find that the less I say in general, the better people listen when I do speak because they know that I won't bother if it's not important.*

When you're determined to get your view understood, you can go on and on and get nowhere. Some women commit communication overkill:

- ▶ Using way too many words
- ▶ Explaining and explaining if the desired response doesn't come
- ▶ Repeating the point until the person shuts down

Your delivery determines whether people tune in or out. When you want to convey a message, don't ignore its vehicle. Which do you prefer—the momentary satisfaction of ragging on someone who tunes out or getting your point across clearly? Joeline says:

After years of keeping quiet, I spoke my mind constantly. But it was very self-absorbed. After working hard to express myself, it was frustrating to feel misunderstood or ignored. When I ranted to a friend, she suggested listening to myself. I blurted out, often demanded my expectations, while criticizing. So I drastically softened my approach.

 NOTE TO SELF: People listen better with their guard down.

Joeline tempered her style and got more. Communicating in a friendly, nag-free tone is more likely to be heard objectively. Do you want revenge or results? To hurt someone or make him or her understand? To vent or get cooperation? Nice Girls on Top have communication skills that get more positive results:

- ▶ *Speak softly.* It helps people listen and see you in control of yourself. People take quiet but firm requests or warnings more seriously.
- ▶ *Don't complain—explain.* If you criticize, insult, whine, nag, lecture, or talk down to someone, the person gets defensive. There's a middle ground between suppressing and being aggressive. State your point in a calm, respectful, and friendly manner, just *explaining* why it bothers you.
- ▶ *Omit personal blame.* "You're as bad as. . . ." Reassure the person that you know he or she didn't do it purposely. "I'm

sure you didn't mean to make me feel this way, but it's how it seems. Can we work together to clear it up?"

▶ *Be specific about what bothers you.* "You aren't fair" is ambiguous. "It's uncomfortable to wait so long on the street when you're late" addresses the issue.

▶ *Choose words carefully.* Give logical examples with kinder words instead of emotional reactions. Insults ("You're so inconsiderate") invite defensiveness. Speaking nicely ("I'd appreciate your not doing that again") is received better. "I'd like to share something with you" is more inviting than "We need to talk."

▶ *Skip excess details or personal issues.* Stick to facts. "Your being late made us miss part of the film." Don't whine about how angry you are.

▶ *Choose a good time to talk.* Bring up problems or set boundaries during a peaceful moment, when you're less angry/more rational, to get less resistance.

▶ *Empathize with the other person's side.* Acknowledge that you understand his or her side to elicit more cooperation. "I know you have a full plate and appreciate your effort."

▶ *Think before blurting what you might regret.* Talking spontaneously might feel good momentarily. But you'll get more mileage out of thinking first. Why annoy someone instead of using a nicer style?

▶ *Call a time-out if things get heated.* When you're each fixed on your own point, suggest a break until you've both cooled down.

▶ *Be direct.* Don't talk around what you want. Be clear. "When can we brainstorm?" vs. "Is it possible to make time to discuss the project?" "Insulting me is unacceptable" vs. "I don't like insults."

▶ *Choose battles wisely.* Don't nitpick every little annoying thing. Focus on what's most important.

▶ *Open and close on a positive note.* Say something kind to lower the other person's guard first. "I value our friendship and want to share something." "I appreciate how hard you work. That's why I want to clear the air about. . . ." End nicely too. "I'm glad I could be straight. Tension isn't good, and I want us to be good."

▶ *Keep it short.* The less said, the greater your chance of being heard. People listen more if you don't ramble on and on.

▶ *Once is enough. Be patient.* Don't repeat yourself to get the desired response. I'd relentlessly press, hoping to be understood. It never worked. Most people hear the first time. They might need time to process, don't know what to say, or feel embarrassed. The person will eventually respond, or not. Leave it alone and change your response.

▶ *Ask for consideration, not change.* You can change only yourself. But you can help someone else understand your side. Explain you'd appreciate more sensitivity to your feelings. "I hate when people say they're coming over but don't" can be "My time is valuable, and I'd appreciate a call to let me know."

▶ *Show appreciation for listening.* Expressing gratitude for the effort to be open-minded gets a better response and a more open ear next time.

▶ *Be clear, not cryptic.* Women are known for saying one thing while meaning another. "It's OK" can mean you're avoiding confrontation.

▶ *Be definite.* Don't dilute your point by presenting it as an opinion. "I think you're being disrespectful" earns less credence than "That's disrespectful." Express it as a fact for more conviction.

EXERCISE: List some of your ongoing complaints. Think of alternative ways to express them and how you can change your behavior to reflect your needs.

ஃ Gently Turning Folks Down ஃ

. . . .

"Never make someone a priority when he
or she only makes you an option."

—SOURCE UNKNOWN

DOES *NO* GET stuck on your lips? Are you afraid of alienating people by not being agreeable? I promise, your tongue won't fall off
if you turn folks down. And you'll enjoy not having an overfilled
plate. You *can* break old habits of saying:

- ▶ yes when you want to say no
- ▶ "no problem" when it's a problem
- ▶ "you can count on me" when you don't want them to

Being selective about whom you give energy to is healthier.
Practice amicably dealing with demands. Yassmin says: "Saying no is hard but can save us a lot of trouble. I would rather save
my energy and time for something with rewards—doing what I
like." I used to give in to everyone when I thought I'd have no life
otherwise. Boy, was I wrong! My life improved tenfold, no, one-
thousand-fold, since I got comfortable with turning people down.
Always agreeing drains you.

Saying No Just Takes Practice

If you're used to fulfilling people's expectations, they may act like
you've let them down. Guilt is manipulation to make you reconsider! Do you believe saying no isn't nice? Remind yourself "I'm
doing nothing wrong by making *me* important." Laurie said in a
group:

I felt powerful when I began saying no to my neighbor, who was always too busy to help me. I didn't know how to turn her down nicely, until you asked if she seemed guilty when she turned me down. She does it easily. Yet there I was, Ms. Okeydokey, with no reason to feel guilty for not doing her bidding! What a powerful awakening. She requests favors like a given. No more being taken for granted! I still help sometimes, but now it's my choice, not duty.

EXERCISE: Pinpoint exactly what makes saying no hard. Are you scared of not being liked, losing the person, looking bad, not seeming nice? Then think hard about whether it's really a terrible thing.

Learn from those who turn you down. Jodee says, "The first time I said no was the hardest. It always is." For People Pleasers, it can be like learning another language. I'd talk to myself and force *no* out. Initially it may not feel exhilarating. People may balk. The first negative reaction made me queasy. But it becomes joyful with practice. Women often say "I can't say no." You can! But the more you affirm you can't, the stronger it becomes your truth. It's your right to prioritize! You *choose* to be agreeable. Now *choose* to stop! Remember:

- ▶ *Don't be apologetic.* Why say you're sorry you can't if you're not? If they hear resolve, they'll accept it; regret, they'll keep asking. Apologies bring more requests.
- ▶ *Make each* no *an individual decision.* For each request, think, "Is this OK for me to do?" If it's not inconvenient, consider it. Find a balance between helping you and helping others.

▶ *Start slowly.* Baby-step, one person at a time, the easiest first. It takes time to break people's habits of expecting your acquiescence.

▶ *Don't succumb to pressure.* People may use guilt and other forms of coercion to change your mind. Sweetly but firmly hold your ground.

▶ *Don't justify.* Don't defend why you can't do something. Men just say they can't. Say it with conviction.

▶ *Be firm in saying no.* Don't dance around it. "I'd love to help, but. . . ." Saying "I can't" tells them to look elsewhere.

 NOTE TO SELF: Saying no doesn't make you a bad person.

It's reasonable to turn down an inconvenient request or something you simply don't want to do. Saying no isn't "not nice." You have the right to value your time and needs. So practice! Anne says:

The best tip my stepmom gave me was the joys of saying no. That it can be done in a gentle and heartfelt way, without offending folks. Even if you're being quick about it, you have the option of saying no for relationships, career work, and everything in between. She said that saying no sometimes prevents the heartache later on when we wish we had said no.

Say "I have the right turn others down!" Do you need permission? Consider it given! Be firm, without saying "I'm sorry," unless you're truly sorry. If you're not, why express unnecessary guilt that dilutes your message? Be firm if the person argues. Get off the phone fast or leave if you're badgered. Set limits and compromise, such as:

- ▶ You can't help all day but can come for two hours
- ▶ You can't run the committee but will participate
- ▶ You're only free in the morning
- ▶ You can't drive her back and forth but can do one way

Saying No Without Saying No

Turn people down without saying no. Create new habits of responding to requests:

- ▶ Pause before responding.
- ▶ Stall. Say you must think about it or check your schedule.
- ▶ Stall more. Ask them to e-mail you. Turning people down electronically is easier.
- ▶ Ponder. Ask, "Do I want to do it or prefer not to?"
- ▶ Excuse yourself. Say you can't do it.

Use expressions like "I can't do it" or "This doesn't work for me." Create pat answers. Flattery can temper refusals. Say you think highly of them but you're overextended. Tell a neighbor you enjoy talking with her but it's not a good time to share family barbecues. If it's more comfortable at first, create excuses. Little white lies ease you into it. Someone calls for a lift—you just washed your hair. Can you come watch her kids? You're writing a report. Survival excuses allow you to bow out nicely. Consistent, reasonable excuses get folks out of the habit of always expecting your help. Agree occasionally. Janis says:

> I always got arguments when I turned Cherise down. She was used to getting her way. I wanted to taper off favors without unpleasantness, so I made excuses she couldn't challenge, like my mom needed me or I had an appointment. Slowly Cherise found other help. Now I just say "I can't" and do an occasional favor.

NOTE TO SELF: *Never* say "I wish I could" unless you want them to rearrange their schedule to grant your wish.

Segue into just saying you can't. Men do. When I began to baby-step out of pleasing mode, I gave elaborate reasons and apologized. Now firmly saying "I can't" invites fewer follow-up requests. My conviction indicates, "Case closed." Robin loves the benefits of her newfound nonacquiescence:

> *I wasn't comfortable saying no and found other ways. My aunt wanted to make a surprise party for my cousin at my place. I said I was too busy and couldn't. It was like dancing. When she prodded about why, I dipped into another direction of conversation. That motivated me to say "I can't" to other things. It's freedom personified! I have more time for what I want!*

Do friends try to rope you into volunteering for charity or at your kids' school? Bow out clearly. Don't be evasive or act regretful. That invites more requests. It's your right to choose how to volunteer. Don't let people with causes intimidate you. Explain that other commitments take all your time—no details—with a smile! A firm attitude reinforces it.

EXERCISE: Find your own version of ways to turn folks down to have handy:

- "That doesn't fit my schedule."
- "Time won't allow me to make more commitments."
- "Filling in when you're away is too important for my limited time."
- "I barely have time to take a potty break with so much on my plate."

"It's Not April Fool's Day, and I'm Still Saying No!"

Some people won't take your new attitude seriously. When I left auto-yes mode, friends suggested I stop kidding. It's normal. But they'll get used to the empowered chick you become! If some don't like it, too bad! Eventually you'll get more respect and know your real friends. As the importance of others decreases and *yours* increases, conviction reinforces it. Michelle says consistency with boundaries helped:

> *I felt hurt that the people I had given so much to in the past could turn on me so quickly, but, realistically, everybody copes differently with change. I think in most cases people lashed out because they didn't understand. I continued to explain where I was coming from, calmly and directly, until they understood. By agreeing to handle certain things over time, I let other people believe they were my responsibility. When I began saying no, there was tension. It has taken time, but, for the most part, people understand where I'm coming from now.*

If you respect others, avoid nastiness, and don't purposely hurt someone, you'll be accepted. People who took advantage may try to get the People Pleaser back. Be strong and proud of holding your ground! Heidi advises, "If done diplomatically, with caring and sharing, they can handle it. Never give more than you can." Consistency helps people adapt. Mala knows it's hard but says it becomes empowering:

> *I told this guy I didn't want to see him anymore. He kept me on the phone for hours, trying to convince me we belonged together, until it finally hit me. Why was I acting as if I needed his consent to end it? I'd said everything that needed to be said. So I said, "I'm sorry you don't agree, but this is the way I feel. I'm hanging up now. Good-bye." With that I hung up the phone. It didn't seem like*

such a "nice girl" thing at the time, but somehow it felt right. I felt proud of myself. Of course, he called right back, but I forced myself not to pick it up.

Don't back down if folks throw guilt or blame their problems on your self-empowerment. That's hogwash! "But you've always done this for me" warrants setting them straight, not compliance. Ask, "Do I still need this person in my life?" It's hard to cut down on favors, but you *can.*

9

Stocking Your Self-Empowerment Toolkit

"There came a time when the risk to remain tight in the bud was more painful than the risk it took to blossom."

—ANAÏS NIN

WHEN YOU DECIDE to take control, the more ammunition you have, the better. This chapter has suggestions for new mind-sets and techniques that can help you handle situations with more ease and grace. Find what works as you gather tools to use for taking a stand nicely. You can use a cool head, courteous attitude, sweet smile, and soft tone to get results that far surpass what most women get.

✍ How to Say It ✍

"If you don't like something, change it. If you can't change it, change your attitude."

—MAYA ANGELOU

PEOPLE PLEASERS ACCEPT feeling unhappy and unfulfilled as a trade-off for keeping the boat steady. Nice Girls on Top rock a little, then a little more, to break old habits. You *can* find more effective ways to handle sticky situations and deal with uncomfortable issues.

Developing an Action Vocabulary

People resist change that's demanded, especially in a critical or angry way. I nicely explain what bothers me—once—then change my response, also nicely. Trust me: actions speak loud and nice behavior confuses folks. As you calmly smile, let your actions make a statement. Emma called after class:

> *Darnell refused to do chores. I needed help with laundry. He grunted and ignored me. I complained as I schlepped to the Laundromat. After class I stopped doing laundry and hand-washed my clothes. Darnell complained about no clean underwear. I smiled. He asked why I had stopped doing laundry. I sweetly explained that while he didn't want to do it, neither did I. We had a standoff. I caught him in the hamper, sniffing. Finally he caved and asked for directions. I thanked him nicely, and it became his chore. Darnell is confused by my sweet attitude and wasn't angry. All because I stopped complaining and spoke with action.*

Smiling when making a point creates a better mood, annoys someone who's pushing buttons to upset you, and defuses negative comments. It's harder to argue with someone who's smiling. People mistake smiling for acquiescence. Show otherwise! Smiling makes people nervous since they know you mean business. Emily says:

When something bothered me, I'd get angry. Then I learned the power of smiling. When Lisa apologized for not returning my call, I calmly said, "I don't like that," and smiled. She apologized as I smiled and said nothing. Ron had the same reaction when he made excuses for not taking the air conditioners from the windows—four weeks in a row. Instead of ranting, I nicely said I accept that he's unreliable and smiled like I'd heard a joke. He got up early the next day and did it! All that energy wasted nagging and complaining.

NOTE TO SELF: Smiling can make people feel guilty, even stupid, for bad behavior.

Show that you won't accept unacceptable behavior. Emily did less for Ron and stopped calling Lisa. All with a smile. And she feels better! Change behavior gradually.

▶ Express what bothers you in a pleasant tone—once. They hear you!
▶ Then do something different if the behavior continues.

Anger makes people defensive, and then they don't learn. Pull back gently, then a bit more. Let the person wonder if you're annoyed. Lambasting them makes bad behavior seem justified: "I'm glad I made her wait. Look how she talks to me." Or validates them: "I was wrong not to call, but too bad. She yelled at me." Speaking sweetly while pulling back makes them rethink behavior. Talia learned:

I realized complaints changed nothing. So I changed. My husband wouldn't call when running late. The kids and I waited impatiently. He laughed. Now we eat without him. The first time he arrived to cold leftovers, he called me vindictive. I laughed and said if he wanted us to wait, he needed to call. Otherwise he could heat up what was left. All said sweetly. He realized he had no right to get angry and my nice delivery allowed no excuse. Now he's prompt or calls.

Don't just threaten! If you tell a friend her behavior is unacceptable, stop accepting it. If you tell your guy you won't stand for his not keeping his word, be prepared to sit if he doesn't—somewhere he isn't! Empty threats get empty results. Gina learned:

My sister used my emergency key to enter my home when I was away. I told her not to. But she did. I yelled to no avail and asked for the key back, but she laughed. So I changed my locks. She was furious, but I nicely explained that she'd left me no choice. Now she takes me seriously when I tell her not to do something.

Silence also sends a message. When people expect to get lectured or criticized and you shut up, they get uneasy. Smile. Don't discuss what annoys you, even if the person tries to. People feel better once they explain or apologize. If you want to get even, don't let them! Accepting apologies helps them move on. Why help? Punish them by not listening. Change the subject when they begin or nicely cut them off with "I've heard it before, so save it." Or use my favorite: "whatever." Not letting them explain or apologize turns guilt inward. Brush them off sweetly: "No need to explain" or "Don't worry about it." Smile and they'll worry more than if you scold!

Turn Confrontation into Communication

Anger instigates a confrontational mind-set, which can rile you. Instead, resolve situations with clear words spoken in a friendly manner. Nice Girls on Top state their intentions nicely, with words and a tone that indicate they expect results. Instead of standing up to someone, think of it as setting limits. Don't raise your voice or snarl. Speaking softly makes people listen harder. Diplomacy—"I understand your point and would like to explain mine"—is more effective than confrontational statements like "You're wrong."

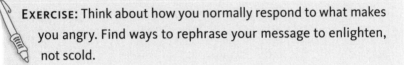

EXERCISE: Think about how you normally respond to what makes you angry. Find ways to rephrase your message to enlighten, not scold.

My operative words are *inappropriate* and *unacceptable*. Depending on circumstances, one or the other gets a point across. Be clear that you expect a situation to be remedied. For example, instead of complaining about your hotel room and asking for another, say "My room is unacceptable. How soon can I move?" Expressing your expectations allows no other options!

▶ "_____ was unacceptable. What compensation will I get?"
▶ "_____ is inappropriate. How will you resolve it?"

Get good results by staying calm. Once your emotions show, you've lost control. In a rational, friendly, but firm tone, explain what you expect and thank the person for cooperating. That shows that you anticipate cooperation. The more nicely you say it, the more positively people respond. Kristie learned:

Something would go wrong, and I'd prepare for battle and attack. On a busy day an annoying co-worker interrupted with a problem she should have handled. I chewed her out and got fired for it. So I adopted Nice Girls on Top skills. I remind myself the person isn't an enemy, which helps me calmly and nicely point out what isn't appropriate. My new boss asked what I do. Everyone wants to work with me because I'm nice! Yet my department is the most efficient. All from nice communication instead of confrontations!

Drop the Desperation

People smell desperation. A disrespectful guy knows you'll hang on, and the boss knows you'll stay with no raise. Being prepared to walk shows. When it's obvious you're serious, you'll get resolution. Lindsay called after our session:

> *I'm a freelance consultant and got scared when business slacked. People took advantage. I'd tell a potential client my fee but consistently get lowballed with "Take it or leave it." I'd take it to pay the rent and feel bitter. You said I created this pattern. People felt my desperation for business. I needed more faith—both spiritually and in myself. I staunchly stood up to the next client. We compromised at a fair amount. Now I walk the walk.*

"Is This Necessary to Share?"

I'm a talkaholic but learned that expressing less gets better results. Some women go on and on. And on. I had to be conscious of keeping that habit under control. Pay attention to details you give folks when you're upset, angry, or frustrated, especially to someone you barely know. Men share fewer details, making it harder for them to tolerate, respond, or listen to excessive sharing, which can create disappointment. I e-mailed many swollen paragraphs about exciting stuff to a male friend. His response? "Cool!" That one word irked me. After I had shared so much, getting one blanket response stank! I reminded myself that he didn't ask for a play-by-play. Now I think first. Courtney laughed when I said this:

People hinted subtly about how much I told them or joked, "Too much information!" A friend finally was straight, saying most people don't care about all the fine points I give and warning it could hurt me at work. I realized I shared too much personal info with my boss and clients. I assumed they wanted to hear if they listened. Now I consider whether it's necessary. Usually it isn't! I just got promoted. My boss said I've changed. All I did was eliminate details from conversations!

 NOTE TO SELF: Before you send an e-mail or speak, think, Is everything necessary?

After being insecure for many years, I realized my old need to impress prompted many details. Paying attention to e-mail correspondence, I often included little bragging or unnecessary facts to show how important or smart or clever I was. Old DoorMat habits die slowly! Now I detail-check and pare correspondence to what's essential. I ask myself, Is this necessary? Whether it's business or personal, keep communication as simple as possible. When I delete something unnecessary, I'm empowered. As someone who talks too much, I love controlling it! Shari e-mailed after a workshop:

I was known for long e-mails and embellishing points with extra info. When you discussed only saying what's necessary, I realized I was out of control. Now I pay close attention to what I write and eliminate everything unnecessary. It's been a kick to feel more in control. Plus, surprisingly, I get faster and more positive responses to e-mails!

Requests and complaints fly better when you keep them simple. Just as I edit books and articles, I edit my communication and
stick to just facts. If you request a certain week for vacation, don't
explain it's because Mom rented a cabin and blah, blah, blah. Just
say you need that week. People don't need to know your personal
business. Grant, who works in customer service for a phone company, says many women give long, personal explanations. Men go
straight to the facts. For example:

WOMAN: *"My phone is out. I expect a call from my daughter who's
traveling. It's given me an upset stomach from worry about miss-
ing calls. Tomorrow I have a meeting at my house and must prepare. What will I do?"*

MAN: *"My phone is dead. When can you fix it? Please forward calls
to my cell."*

I used to ramble about how inconvenienced I was, without
addressing getting resolution. Customer service people don't need
to hear about the problems. It's annoying. Grant says when someone runs on about all the repercussions of a problem, he wants
to rush off the phone. It's inappropriate, and you get less service.
Grant explains:

*Women complain way too much. I don't have to know who might
call them. A plumber doesn't need to know what she was doing
when the toilet stuffed up. It's unnecessary and wastes time that
could be used to fix the problem. It's hard to work with someone
like that. If women would learn to get to the point fast, they'd get
better service.*

Stick to the facts! 'Nuff said?

Where Politeness Ends

Girls are taught to be polite. What does that mean? Accepting behavior you don't like? Agreeing with what you don't want? Letting people intrude? Redefine *polite*! It doesn't mean being obligated to everyone. When salespeople call, do you listen politely? Why? You didn't give permission to be disturbed, so why listen to a sales pitch? I quickly say, "I'm not interested. I'm hanging up." And do! That's polite enough. You owe nothing.

Has someone talked your ears off when you were stuck, like during a haircut? Don't listen to problems or opinions. Nicely explain that you'd like quiet:

▶ "I was looking forward to sitting in peace after a hectic week."
▶ "I know you'll understand I just want to chill and listen to music."

You're not obligated to listen. On a plane, if someone babbles, I smile, open a magazine or my laptop, or put on headphones. It's not rude not to talk to strangers. They're rude to insist. Uncomfortable situations call for polite boundaries. Sue says:

I went for lunch in a pensive mood and wanted to be alone. My waiter was friendly. I politely said I wasn't in the mood to talk. He continued, asking why a pretty woman like me was sitting by myself. I nicely asked him to do his job—take my order and nothing else. He got an attitude but shut up. I felt powerful.

 NOTE TO SELF: Do what you want, not what you think politeness mandates.

This is a *big* one. Don't let men put you on the spot. Some prey on women who try to be courteous. Ignore them! They approach under a friendly guise and hit on you in ways crafted to instill guilt if you don't respond. Don't be intimidated or make excuses to end it. Or let them play the "just being nice" card. You have no obligation to respond to strangers. Period. If you didn't invite him over, no explanation is needed. His annoyance is *his* problem. If women consistently stopped succumbing to intrusions, men would learn not to interrupt and expect attention. Quickly and firmly brush them off.

◈ How to Solve Problems ◈

. . . .

"Even if you're on the right track, you'll get
run over if you just sit there."

—WILL ROGERS

YOU HAVE THE power to control your circumstances! Use subtle tactics. Give people the benefit of the doubt. They may not know you find them rude or inappropriate. Explain your position nicely. Jessica learned:

> *After class I prepared to set boundaries and express myself. I was pleasantly surprised to discover they didn't know how I felt. Mom said her mom had called at work every day, so she did too. She agreed to limit calls. A neighbor thought my unlocked door meant it was okay to enter without knocking. Now she knocks. Some friends didn't respond well. I'm slowly educating them. But some success is good! Wish I'd spoken up sooner instead of feeling anger toward people for things they didn't know bothered me.*

EXERCISE: Build your nerve, by writing your answers to these questions:
- ➤ What are the benefits of your not standing up for yourself?
- ➤ Do you like feeling powerless? Does subservience feel good?
- ➤ What scares you about speaking up?
- ➤ How would your life be better if you transformed into a Nice Girl on Top?

Trying New Techniques

Nice Girls on Top techniques work better than People Pleasing or being tough/overtly assertive. Adopt appropriate ones for each situation that, until now, you confronted head-on or ignored to keep the peace. Try to:

▶ *Address problems without getting personal.* Stick to facts with a positive spin. Focus on actions and situations instead of the person. You'll be heard more objectively.

- ➤ "You did it wrong" can be "Let's discuss other ways to do it."
- ➤ "You were nasty" can be "Your words made me feel. . . ."

▶ *Ask for suggestions about how to handle someone's nonsense instead of complaining ineffectively.* People hate complaints, but many folks like giving advice. So explain the problem without sounding like you're complaining, say something nice about the person you're talking about, and solicit suggestions for handling it. Now they're working with you to determine a solution. Chandra found it effective:

My sisters and I spent a weekend with Mom and Dad. I get along with Melissa, but Lauren, the baby, ignores boundaries. Mom hates complaints. Lauren went through my things to borrow my iPod, which I'd said no to. Later I was furious when she wore my dress! Instead of ranting to Mom and Melissa, I calmly asked for suggestions for setting boundaries with Lauren without creating static. I explained we're all adults and why it bothered me. Speaking nicely helped them see my side. We all talked to Lauren. If I had had my usual rant about it, they'd have sided with Lauren. But asking for their help worked!

▶ *Express appreciation for someone's cooperation instead of demanding it.* It makes people more likely to agree. Bitches demand; People Pleasers hint or ask quietly. Nice Girls on Top explain their needs so they make sense. Men are especially receptive to requests with explanations. Many need to understand why before agreeing. Just saying with a pout "Because I want it" won't get cooperation, unless you're prepared to buy him with sex.

 NOTE TO SELF: Compliments disarm folks and ease tensions.

▶ *Address problems using honey.* I hate saying this, but flattery is a fantastic tool for softening negative interactions. Compliments lower people's guards, making them more receptive. Say something nice before confronting problems. Stoking egos gets folks on your side, especially at work. Say how you admire her accomplishments or you've learned a lot from him. Robin says:

I look for nice things to say to people who give me a hard time or have something I need. I saw a friend I'd stood up to, immediately gave her a compliment, and saw her hostility melt. I had to leave work early when my boss needed me. The next day I brought coffee and told him how much I respect his ability to deal with people. He forgave me. If someone is annoyed, I find something nice to say. It can make the person easier to deal with.

▶ *Show empathy for the person's situation or inability to do something.* People take criticism or suggestions better if you acknowledge believing they don't mean harm, even if you believe they do. Attacking makes people defensive. Instead, begin with "I know you don't mean to make me feel unappreciated, but when you ____, that's how I feel." Acknowledge their situation. "I don't know how you manage all the work. I appreciate your listening and need to address. . . ." They'll listen with more objectivity!

▶ *Always speak in private.* Wait until you're alone to address problems. Sometimes people need to maintain a front when others are watching that gets dropped in private if you speak nicely and show interest in resolving the issue. Explain that you're speaking one-on-one out of respect for them.

▶ *Ask for suggestions for resolving an issue from the person you have the issue with.* Telling someone what bothers you and demanding your way rarely gets good results. Instead, ask how the person causing your problem suggests you handle the situation and work together for a solution. It puts you on the same side. Begin by saying something nice, then:

- Tell Mom you hate losing your temper when she nags. Can she suggest what you could do when she pushes you too far? Leave the room? Put a sock in her mouth (joking!)? Say something over and over?
- Tell your guy you don't want to nag, so what can you do instead? Chain him to his workbench (joking)? Ask at a different time or in a different way?

- Tell your assistant you don't want to keep pushing her to work and to stop personal e-mails and long breaks. What should you do? Increase her work hours? Dock her pay? Fire her? Or can she please work with you?

▶ *Use humor.* I included some jokes in the preceding comments. Joking can get a point across in ways the person can accept with better spirit than a complaint.

The Most Annoying Types

Some people push others' buttons especially well. As discussed in Chapter 3, they hurt others when they're in pain. Muster the compassion to deal with them with more finesse. Compassion is a lubricant for a happy life. People have reasons. Unloving mothers raise unloving children who become unloving adults. Accepting that behavior results from past pain can help you stop taking it personally. Feel sorry for them instead of reacting angrily or feeling wounded. That puts power in your court instead of giving them power over your feelings.

A positive perspective makes dealing with annoying people easier. Thinking they're mean and rotten makes you antagonistic. If you approach them as nice people whose behavior is shaped by old hurts or insecurity, you'll have a better attitude. Take control— nicely, with a smile—when you meet these types:

CRITICS. Some people criticize. They're usually unhappy. Maybe they were insulted as kids, so now they give it back. Be compassionate when people find fault in what you say or do. Don't take it personally! They probably look for thorns in a bouquet of roses. Make a friendly comment, with a smile, such as:

► "You must really like me if you pay so much attention. Thanks!"
► "Why does it bother you if it doesn't bother me?"
► "I'm sorry you don't like that about me, but I do, so it's OK."

BUTTINSKIES. Some folks pry into personal affairs or are downright nosy. "How much do you make?" "What did you pay for ____?" Don't answer! Change the topic. Are you asked when you'll marry or have kids? Don't get defensive! People get stupid under the guise of caring. Be vague. Or say directly, with a smile:

► "We're very happy as we are."
► "Is it a problem for you? It isn't for us."
► "Dad taught me not to ask those kind of questions, so I don't answer them."
► "I'd rather not answer that. I hope you understand it's private."

ONE-WAY TAKERS. Some folks have a distorted sense of entitlement. They might expect help to enter your field. People call or e-mail me "to pick your brain" about my profession and think I'm obligated to answer. I don't! If I always agreed, my brain would be shredded, and I wouldn't have time for paying clients. Set boundaries. Does a friend borrow clothes, which are returned stained, or expect you to design a free logo even though it's your livelihood? A neighbor may dump kids on you for regular "emergencies." Set them all straight—nicely. They'll keep taking otherwise.

► "My plate is too full to help."
► "Please ask in the future instead of assuming you can ____."
► "My fee for doing that starts at $____."

FAT POLICE. Some folks, usually with their own body image issues, notice every ounce you gain or lose. I'd get a complex visiting certain people who fixated on my weight, making me self-conscious. I recognized that it reflected their insecurities, had compassion, and stopped it, with a friendly tone:

▶ "Why does my weight matter to you so much? I'm fine with my body."
▶ "I know you don't enjoy making me feel bad, but you do by pointing out extra pounds."
▶ "Do you like anything about me? It would be nice to hear that too."

SHOW-OFFS/NARCISSISTS. Some folks think the world revolves around them. Grrrr . . . Makes ya just want to smack 'em! Use compassion instead. They often don't have fulfilling relationships. Former unattractive, poor achievers, etc., who became swans need to remind everyone, "Look at me, I'm gorgeous; smart; successful." Insecure folks are self-focused, braggers, or name-droppers. Feel sorry for those whose identity is what they've done or whom they know. It's hard to believe that gorgeous and successful people can be insecure. I've counseled many. When you feel good about you, bragging isn't necessary. I avoid narcissists or set them straight—nicely—with:

▶ (Jokingly) "Wow, you're so amazing I don't know why you talk to me."
▶ "It would be nice if you'd give me a turn to talk."
▶ "Are you interested in what I'm doing?"
▶ "You've made it clear how wonderful you are. Thanks."

KNOW-IT-ALLS. Some folks—Mom, friends, co-workers, et al—live to give unsolicited advice. At work they instruct you about software you already know. They advise you how to raise your kids; why you should wear makeup; how to walk, talk, and breathe. They interrupt to finish your sentence. You want to say "Mind your own business," scream you're smart enough to handle it, etc. Have compassion. Often they don't realize it. They're probably insecure and need to feel useful. Say thanks but:

- ▶ "I value your wanting to help but know what I'm doing."
- ▶ "I'll keep that in mind if I need it."
- ▶ "We have a difference of opinion, but I'm going to work with mine, thanks."
- ▶ (For ongoing advice) "I know you mean well, but when you keep telling me what to do it feels like you think I'm incompetent. That doesn't feel good, so I'd appreciate your being more aware of that." (Smile!)

10

Living as a Nice Girl on Top

"There are two ways of meeting difficulties: you alter the difficulties, or you alter yourself to meet them."

—PHYLLIS BOTTOME

*I*T'S TIME TO thrive in the real world! Shed your People Pleaser armor for confidence and satisfaction. In this chapter, I'll show you how to put Nice Girls on Top techniques into action in many common situations. Prepare to control your life!

❧ Holding Your Ground ❧

"He that will not apply new remedies must expect new evils."

—FRANCIS BACON

Before taking a stand, ask, "Am I willing to be serious?" You may want to stop unacceptable behavior, but are you willing to leave or mean no or cut visits if ignored? Decide how far you're willing to go. If you can't cut the person off, have less contact. Explain what bothers you and why you'll limit visits. Don't demand change. It comes when people are aware of how their behavior affects you and want to work with you. I'll discuss common situations and how to navigate them.

Practice new techniques for handling situations. No one has a right to be disrespectful or consistently burst your happiness bubble. No one! Your mother has no right to cut you down. Your best friend's issues aren't yours. It isn't mandatory to take crap from your boss. A romantic partner has no special right to abuse you, even if he says it's your fault—which it never is! In this chapter you'll find examples of effective alternatives.

> **EXERCISE:** Before you begin to take control of situations:
>
> - Do affirmations to bolster your confidence. "I have the right to express what bothers me." "I trust myself to communicate effectively."
> - Remember that nicely discussing problems makes relationships—professional or personal—stronger.
> - Reread the communication tips in Chapter 8.
> - Use deep breathing to keep emotions in check.
> - Face the reality of a situation and choose to walk away or change your response.

With Friends, Family, and Acquaintances

Complaints to friends, family, and acquaintances often don't work. *That's reality.* Stop complaining and respond differently, avoid them, or stop dealing. Getting aggravated and complaining doesn't help, does it? LaTonya says:

> *I was always mad at someone. I'd repeat that it was disrespectful not to call about tentative plans, ignore me when they had some-*

one else to hang with, or not replace what they had borrowed and
lost. I was a good victim. When I faced reality and accepted that
unless I acted different they'd keep on keeping on, I stopped feeling
helpless and nicely explained I wouldn't tolerate this anymore. My
sister got angry when I wouldn't make plans, but she saw I meant
it and asked for another chance. I feel more respect from friends
and family now that I respect myself enough to set boundaries!

If she's always late, it's *your* choice to wait. *That's reality.* Explain that you'll leave after ten minutes—and leave! If he expects you to accompany him to work events but ignores yours, stop going. If she often cancels at the last minute, stop making plans. If he forgets—again—to return tools you lent months ago, don't lend them again. *That's reality.* If she repeats a confidence, explain that you're disappointed, accept that she has a big mouth, and keep yours shut. *That's reality!* Some women forget friends when they have a boyfriend but expect support after breaking up. Accept lapses in friendship or be busy. *That's reality.* People Pleasers keep calling and get aggravated. Natasha stopped:

I got tired of complaining that friends didn't call as promised.
They'd shrug it off. One actually said she isn't the type to call and
friends call her. How convenient! I'd seethe inside but call. Eventu-
ally I nicely said that while I respect her right not to call, I wasn't
the type always to initiate and stopped calling. She eventually
picked up the phone.

NOTE TO SELF: Don't be angry when folks do what they always do. Change your response!

Do you go out with someone who gets drunk and embarrassing or is desperate for a guy? It's hard to watch a friend act foolishly or make sleazy moves and you feel sleazy by association. Explain that being her caretaker isn't fun. Ask to do lunch instead. If she balks, balk back more firmly. Lauren says:

Mya is a great friend but parties hard. I don't. When we went out, she'd drink and get crazy—dance on tables, grind against guys, embarrassing me. I explained I couldn't party anymore and invited her for dinner. We enjoyed chatting and watching videos. Now that's what we do.

Do friends get mad when you don't meet their needs? LaVonne complained in a group that her friend thought they should do everything together and got angry if LaVonne made plans without her, throwing fits to manipulate her. I encouraged setting boundaries and keeping them. She reported:

I told Cali I wouldn't feel obligated to her in all my plans. She cut an attitude and called me selfish. I said she was the selfish one. She stormed off. It was the first time I'd stood up to her. I haven't heard from her and feel terrible, but I'm following instructions and not apologizing. It feels good to make plans freely.

LaVonne asked if she should initiate amends. The group yelled, "No!" She'd done nothing wrong. Friendship needs boundaries when one person expects more than the other. LaVonne felt bad after two weeks. I advised e-mailing Cali to suggest having dinner, without mentioning what happened. Cali agreed and slowly accepted boundaries.

There's a big difference between being a good friend and having to ignore your own needs to satisfy a friend's need. Cali needed constant company, but LaVonne didn't want to feel obligated to be her constant companion. LaVonne had a right to do activities or make plans without her. Being a good friend also doesn't mean having to be brought down by listening to the same complaints, day after day, about problems and unhealthy situations that your friend consistently creates by making poor choices or refusing to take action to change. Be there if a friend needs to talk or complain about what bothers her, without shoving advice on her that she doesn't want. But it shouldn't be at your expense. Don't make her problems yours!

If a friend's problem or complaint becomes a lifestyle, decide if you want to continue to listen to the same whine whenever you talk. If you don't, then refuse to discuss it, seriously cut back on your communication, or end the friendship, as discussed in Chapter 5. Show empathy and acknowledge when someone is having a rough time. But if she calls you a bad friend for halting her complaints about the same boyfriend, her work situation, or her mom driving her crazy, explain that you've made suggestions and listened to the same complaints for a long time and that since she chooses to do nothing, you'd rather not keep discussing her abusive boyfriend or the roommate who consistently messes up her apartment. Lindsay says:

> *Maggie went in circles with the same problems. When I made suggestions, she called me critical. After years of my listening to her whine about needing to clean her apartment and charge more for her services, she exploded when I said she needed to take action. We stopped talking, and I'm relieved. I can't watch her self-destruct.*

Do you get held hostage on the phone? Get folks used to shorter calls! Explain that you'll just say a quick hello as you're leaving or with someone. A diplomatic line is "Let me let you go." If she resists, get firmer or call your number from another phone. When call-waiting beeps, jump off. Consistency breaks long phone habits. Explain that you enjoy speaking but need to keep calls shorter since you're busy. Ali says:

> *The more I've developed a life, the less I want to chat endlessly. Some friends talk for hours. I'd grit my teeth. Now I'm honest. My sister got angry, saying I don't make enough time for her. I explained that I talk a lot at work and need quiet time. She called me selfish. I said her demands for time I couldn't spare were selfish. It hurt our relationship, but she's getting used to it. We meet for coffee or dinner to catch up.*

Living in your sphere doesn't entitle anyone to take advantage. Does a neighbor park in your space, borrow without asking, etc., and make excuses? You're not the neighborhood weenie for speaking up—the space-stealer is! Does she call you petty or unfriendly? Don't succumb. Maintain your position nicely:

- ▶ "Why are you making me the bad guy when you took my ____?" Smile!
- ▶ "Please ask before using my ____. I appreciate your cooperation!" More smiles!

People take advantage, knowing it's uncomfortable to confront neighbors. State your case softly but firmly. Beth complained that Pat's daughter Britney was a sneaky bully who picked on her daughter Liza. Beth knew Pat thought Britney was an angel. I suggested using the asking-for-advice technique. Beth says:

> *I invited Pat for coffee. Instead of complaining, I explained that there seemed to be a problem between our girls. Liza wasn't sure why, but Britney seemed mad. I fought the urge to barf when I said Britney was a lovely girl and I hoped they could be friends. I shared things Britney had done—only when she asked. My focus was on*

their friendship, not the bullying. I watched my words, explaining some of the actions, without negative adjectives. Pat took it well and talked to Britney. Now she picks on someone else.

Pat was more receptive because Beth didn't criticize her daughter. The concern about Britney and Liza's friendship made them allies in resolving the problem instead of Pat's feeling like an adversary and getting defensive. Beth and Pat continue to get along. While Liza doesn't like Britney, Beth encourages her to be friendly.

When I did substitute teaching, I never had trouble getting a parent's cooperation. Regular teachers wondered how I got more support from parents than they could. Simple! I didn't complain. I expressed concern that Tim's behavior affected his work. Mrs. A said, "Tim disrupts the class, and I waste time disciplining. You must do something." I'd say, "I want to see Tim do well, so let's work together to settle him down to get better grades." Every parent responded well! I empathized with how hard discipline was. Mrs. A continued whining that I must have magic powers. Nicely asking to work together is more effective.

Roommates create special problems. Lecturing won't help. Either set firm boundaries, find a new roommate, or leave. *That's reality!* Years ago mine left dirty dishes, often for days, after persistently being asked nicely to wash them. So I put them in a bag outside. He got angry, but I sweetly explained our potential roach problem. After that he washed them! I had an up-front rule for roommates: "If it's not yours, don't touch." Set boundaries before living together and choose your battles. Janet shared in a support group:

My roommate Carol is irresponsible. She'd promise many things but not follow through. I believe in honoring your word and got angry. Carol does as she pleases. We didn't get along until I forced myself to accept how she is. Now I concern myself only with what directly affects me. When she promises, I have few expectations. I do expect things like rent and made it clear if she can't honor them, she's out. We discuss instead of my lecturing and get along better. I enjoy her nice qualities since we understand each other.

With Money Pigs

Money issues can create sticky problems. Nora complained about Cathy in class:

She borrows money without repaying. She's always short a few dollars when we go out. I usually have to kick in something for her dinner, movie, or cab. She forgets to return it. I get angry but still lend money. I don't know how to stop.

I told Nora to bring just enough for herself and let Cathy handle it, like finding a cash machine or washing dishes! Nora took that as permission. People Pleasers worry about being unaccommodating. Accommodate *you*. Nora called to say Cathy used emergency money in her wallet when refused financial aid. She couldn't believe Cathy would let her pay to keep that money. It's not your responsibility if someone doesn't bring enough. Warn a friend in advance that you know she runs short but you won't have extra, or you two can go somewhere cheaper.

Do you have money pig friends who always order extras yet expect to split the check? These oinkers manipulate to afford lots of drinks or appetizers. People Pleasers are embarrassed to speak up and end up paying too much. Nice Girls on Top won't subsidize them. Lori shared in class that her friend Jess takes advantage:

At dinner she orders more drinks and expensive food than anyone, then grabs the check and divides it so everyone shares her tab. I *don't drink and eat light while she has steak. I've paid over $20 more than my meal at times! I want to just pay for my order but hate being called cheap. She did that to someone who protested. Jess gets nasty, so we all pay. I wish I had the nerve to protest.*

Money pigs should be embarrassed! I had dinner with a friend who arrived early to have drinks and appetizers. I had a salad and water. She had more drinks and side dishes with dinner. The $40 check had many items, so she said it was easier to just split it. I asked her how complicated it was to subtract my $7 salad from the bill since the rest was hers. She was annoyed I didn't contribute to her tab. She'd done it before—no more! If a friend gets angry if you don't subsidize her, stop making plans. Nice Girls on Top don't succumb to guilt. Whitney taught someone a lesson:

Nancy often complained about her friend Marie, who had big meals and several drinks yet put everyone on the spot to split the check. When she said Marie would join us for her birthday dinner, I warned her to tell Marie I'd pay for half of Nancy's dinner and my own. Marie ordered extravagantly and insisted she and I split the check. I just gave my share. Marie ordered $45 more than me! She pulled the "I don't have enough money" card. I said she shouldn't order more than she could pay for. The restaurant didn't take credit cards, but I wouldn't relent. Nancy put in $45 for her own birthday dinner! Marie tried to make me feel guilty, but I said she should feel guilty. I felt bad for Nancy but had warned her. She couldn't stand up to Marie, but I wouldn't pay for it.

NOTE TO SELF: If someone calls you cheap for not splitting the check, ask what she calls herself for always expecting others to subsidize her.

Be honest with someone who takes advantage. Explain that you don't want to share a check when she always orders more. On the other hand, don't be cheap and count pennies if it's a small difference or if sometimes you have more and sometimes she does. You can win the money pigs' game. Try:

▶ *Best* way: Figure out what your share is before the check arrives. Have it ready and say "This is what I owe."
▶ Ask for separate checks.
▶ If someone says "Let's split the check," say you'd like to just pay your share.

With Parents

Reality: *Parents often see with different vision because they adhere to older values.*

It can be frustrating to fight with parents. Clients ask why their parents can't accept them. Since they were brought up differently, they view actions through the eyes of their limited mentality—parent glasses! If they don't understand what you're doing, it may seem wrong. *That's reality.* Work from that reality instead of fighting to make them see your way. You *can* get along with your parents.

> **NOTE TO SELF:** The best way to deal with the reality of parents is to accept that they may never see your way, and that's OK.

Stop trying to make your parents understand what they refuse to. Arguing doesn't help, so why bother? Change *your* response and attitude. Explain, since you love them and want to get along, that you'll accept the fact that they don't understand you. Could they accept your right to think and act differently? Speak in a loving, noncritical way. Sara learned:

> *My parents and I were always at odds, until I accepted that they won't change their thinking and would never understand my lifestyle and didn't need to. I avoided hot topics and stopped getting angry when they got on my case about something they can't understand. We discussed our different ways of thinking and together set boundaries. When we begin a lose/lose argument, I change the subject. Since I approached our problems from a place of love instead of anger, we get along much better!*

If you express feelings to a critical parent to no avail, save your energy. Try to understand where it comes from. Parents often want their kids to do better than they did or live out dreams they couldn't or avoid failures by doing what they see as right. What they lay on you may actually reflect self-criticism. You don't advance at work? Maybe Dad feels like a failure. No husband? Maybe Mom gets badgered about why you're not married. Consider their history. Find the compassion not to erupt or melt down from critical comments. They may reflect discontent. Debbie says:

> *I often fought with my parents. They pushed me to fix little flaws that infuriated me. When you asked about their parents, I watched Grandpa's (Dad's father) behavior. He orders Dad and Grandma around. Dad bristles but tries to please his father. Grandpa questions him about me. Dad pushes me to be perfect. What a revelation! Dad picks on me because of Grandpa. Mom goes along, like her mother. It's easier to feel compassion.*

There can be special static between mothers and daughters. Some moms think it's their right to tell you what to do. Mom might envy your successes if she has none or want to spare you disappointments by changing in you what she dislikes in herself—overweight, settling for what you get, etc. You're always her child, even at forty or sixty. Parents get protective. That's normal. They also butt in unfairly and think they know best, even if you disagree. That's normal too. It's frustrating when parents fuss over you. Try to remember it's their nature to protect. You're still a kid in their eyes.

I finally accepted that my mom was brought up to please and couldn't relate to my independent ways and never would. Patience, love, and kindness helped us get along better. Accepting that Mom acted from love nurtured my patience. Instead of losing your temper, lovingly tell Mom that you appreciate the love behind her desire to run your life, but you're an adult and need to make your own choices. She taught you well and is a good source of advice if needed. "Can you please let me find my own way?" Recognize that she'll never accept everything you do and that's OK. Kelly says:

Everything Mother suggested used to tick me off. I saw her as trying to run my life. She saw me as an ungrateful daughter to refuse her wisdom. I thought about her giving up college and career to marry Dad and be a stay-at-home mother. With Peg and me grown, Mom feels useless. She was a good mother, and I understand her need to help. Now I ask for advice, and she bugs me less. We must get beyond the surface to understand what's going on to find ways to adjust problems.

EXERCISE: Practice gently saying a version of "When you tell me what to do, I feel like you don't respect me as an adult. That doesn't feel good." Use it when a parent bugs you.

Losing your temper keeps the cycle going. By responding differently to parents, you can help break annoying habits. Tell Mom you love her and don't like arguing. Without animosity or criticism, or saying she's wrong, explain that since you may never understand each other's point of view, "Let's stop trying to force it on each other." Ask to stop talking about topics that push each other's buttons. Emphasize you know she doesn't mean to annoy you. Try some caring phrases to get her on your side:

▶ "Let's find a way to get along better!"
▶ "I know you're trying to help because you love me, but I'm an adult and make my own decisions. Please respect that."
▶ "I don't want to hurt your feelings but must do what feels best for me."

Address issues in a calm, loving, nonaccusing tone. She may counter that what she does isn't terrible. Make it clear that even if she doesn't mean to make you feel bad, she does. Can she be more sensitive? Be nice but firm. If she won't take you seriously, explain that you'll have to avoid her in situations that she makes too uncomfortable. Ask Mom for suggestions on dealing with those situations. If things get heated, suggest you stop and continue later. Mimi's mom finally got it when she clearly explained:

Mom always pointed out my need to lose weight. I complained. She said it's a mother's duty to help me be happy. During a good moment I asked if she really wanted me to be happy. "Of course!" So I explained how unhappy I felt when she picked on me. I can see myself and don't need her constant reminders of my struggle with weight. It's my choice to eat something fattening and unnecessary to embarrass me at family gatherings and ruin my day. She was shocked and tries to stop. I never thought it could happen, but talking to her nicely, as one adult to another, got through!

If she regularly does certain things—picks on something sensitive, talks to you like a child, or embarrasses you with others—nicely ask her to please reconsider before she speaks. If she offers to stop, suggest a private word signal or line to repeat as a reminder if she does it. The more loving your words, the more cooperation. Make it simple, such as "Remember your promise." Don't argue. Repeat it like a mantra, calmly, until she stops. I used to say, "Mom, remember. . . ." It worked beautifully. Chaundra tried:

Since childhood, Mama talked about me in front of others like I wasn't there. "Ignore Chaundra if she talks too much." "Chaundra tells long stories." It was embarrassing! I told her to stop, but she thought I was silly. After your workshop I invited her for coffee. Calmly I explained why her comments embarrass me and got through! She didn't think it mattered much, but my noncritical explanation made sense. She promised to stop. I asked what to say if she began. She suggested, "Mama, you're doing it." I say it without anger, and she stops. My sister couldn't believe it the first time! We get along much better!

Some parents overdo concern. Does Mom insist you check in daily? Slowly wean her off that. Call a little less. Don't apologize. She'll continue to expect it if you do. Explain you love her but are busy. Don't take her calls on your cell or rush to return them. If parents get too nosy, thank them for caring but nicely explain you need privacy as an adult. Moms can be obsessed about babies. Resist overreacting. Your mother may be getting pressure from friends. Calmly acknowledge you know she wants the best for you and you're happy as is for now. You love her but get upset when she hounds you. Ask for patience and respect for your right to choose. If she persists, calmly respond, "I've explained my feelings and would appreciate your respecting them."

Mothers-in-law can be more difficult than moms. Enlist your husband's support to set boundaries. When I was married, I swore I'd never directly cause a rift between him and his mom. If there was a problem, he addressed it and supported me. But you need to be reasonable. If you nitpick everything, it's harder for your guy to support you. Stand up for what matters most. Robin says:

> *My husband's mother is a shrew—always sarcastic to me. I avoid being alone with her. When she gets my blood boiling, my husband sets her straight. She once got exceptionally nasty. I told my husband we were leaving and wouldn't return unless she was kept in check. He talked to his dad, and they both stood up to her. She was better for a while.*

When you have kids, parents and in-laws can be more intrusive about visits. Gently set limits. They won't like it, but you're entitled to space. Madge says:

> *Mom expected us to get her and Dad every Friday and drive them home Sunday. It's too much. We want time alone. Plus, my in-laws live nearby and think they can come without calling. They interrupt Brady's nap. We need downtime. So we told our parents we'd see them less often. My parents could spend one weekend a month here. Sometimes we visit for a day. My in-laws said it was silly to call first. Now my front door is locked and we don't answer when they come. They got angry, but we explained if they wouldn't respect our privacy, we'd take it. Now they call and grudgingly accept when it's not a good time.*

People take more abuse from family members. Cut family slack, but if someone makes you miserable, take action! Some parents abuse children or are unkind. If a family member is abusive or hurtful, distance yourself. Family obligation doesn't mean accepting cruelty, even if they say it's for your good. If you feel bad, it's not good! See them less. And less. If they ask why, be truthful. If that creates more grief, curtail contact, or the damage can be great. Michelle learned:

> *My father can be outspoken, intimidating, and "always right." Spending my childhood trying to make him happy (the impossible dream) still affects me. I'm just learning to trust myself. Trying to make my father proud and not being able to was a source of shame for a long time. I spent my first twenty years having "conversations" where he asked and answered his own questions and can't remember ever having the courage to really talk about my feelings or opinions. Recently I decided it was important to let him know I'd been hurt by him. I explained that I had spent my childhood feeling intimidated and was capable of more than he thought. He spoke over me, but I literally kept repeating myself. I did this twenty times before he actually took it in. He got angry, but the next time I saw him he asked my opinion about things. He still wishes I was a nanny and engaged to a nice Latin American boy making six figures as a doctor, but it's a start.*

Keep calls to annoying parents brief. If you get verbal abuse, explain that you can't listen, say good-bye, and hang up. In person, say "I love you but must leave. Your words hurt." Parents have no right to tear down their children. Your duty isn't to quietly be injured. It's normal to want parental approval. But sometimes it just won't happen. *That's reality.* Accept it or waste energy trying to please them and get snagged when it doesn't happen.

NOTE TO SELF: While it's good to be kind to parents, it's unkind to let them hurt you.

Reality: *Childhood patterns continue until your response changes them.* Accept that your parents may never understand you. Stop trying to convince them you're right. It just causes aggravation. Don't act childlike with them. You may not realize you do, but pay attention to your voice. Are you defensive? Speak as an adult— respectfully—even if they don't reciprocate. Relationships change slowly as you all get used to new communication. Don't do the Mommy dance—verbal sparring she provokes. It's never satisfying, so why bother? Be loving and compassionate instead!

While boundaries are important, if Mom and Dad are seniors, have compassion. Call regularly, listen for a few minutes, and know you've given a blessing. If they've been good parents, make time. When my mom got older, I always took her calls, especially after my dad passed. She had a knack for catching me deep in work. But I know it's hard to get old and feel helpless and lonely. Despite frustration at getting interrupted during work-intensive moments, I wanted to be there for Mom, as she always was for me. That wasn't being a DoorMat. I was returning her love. When I lost her, I felt blessed to have helped her through tough years.

With Customer Service People

Do you complain about customer service people? If you were brought up to avoid causing problems, you may keep your mouth shut about bad service or defective products and complain to friends. Reaching a person instead of an automated voice can be exasperating and put you in a bad mood. Irritability attracts poor service! Instead, force a smile, even if they can't see it, since it sets a better mood. Then nicely seek resolution.

I confess. I get phenomenal service—refunds few get, courtesy, direct phone numbers for future problems, replacement products, and apologies—all because they appreciate my being nice. I got poor service when I was scared of offending someone whose job was to help me. But resentment built, and my emotions and frustrations made me rant and whine, making them less helpful. Such anxiety for what you're entitled to! Nice Girls on Top approaches get much better service.

▶ *Know you're entitled to assistance with what you pay for.* Show that in your attitude.

▶ *Be friendly.* Calm down before calling. Rudeness relieves momentary tension but won't create an ally for solving your problem. Friendly and polite makes the person try harder for you.

▶ *Don't share personal problems or sob stories.* Just nicely state the facts and what you'd like.

▶ *Explain that your patience is thin and you're upset.* Admit it's been frustrating. Use humor, such as "I'm trying to stay calm. How am I doing?" That gets the person on your side to see you as human, instead of another complainer.

▶ *Acknowledge that the person didn't cause your problem.* If your statement is wrong, your phone is dead, or you have some other typical problem, the customer service person didn't cause it. Don't take anger out on her or scold him. I open with a version of "I know you didn't break my phone and are trying to help me. I'll try not to take my anger out on you and appreciate your help." They greatly appreciate that!

▶ *Whether verbal or written, don't jump into a complaint.* Begin with a kind word to set a positive tone and say you're surprised you had this bad experience. You want to remain a customer.

▶ *Use clear, unemotional words about why you need resolution.* "I get crazy when my phone is out" brings out violins. "I'm losing business without phone service" is taken more seriously.

▶ *Let the person know it's in the company's best interest to correct the problem.* Explain that action you may take isn't worth their ignoring your situation.

▶ *Respond firmly to lines used to get rid of you.* To "It's not our
policy to _____," I reply, "It's not my policy to accept faulty service or a customer service department that tries to brush me
off." Sweetly, with a smile.

Some women need to build courage to ask for what they should
get. You're a customer they make money from! Get into the driv-
er's seat. Being tough is unnecessary. Service people hear many
rants and threats. Friendliness, with humor, makes them like you
more and go the distance. I chat and joke, while reminding them
how important it is to get resolution. A snail mail letter works better than an e-mail complaint. Keep it short and sweet, literally—a
few paragraphs using my tips. Be polite and don't accuse. Just state
the problem and ask how they can fix it.

NOTE TO SELF: When you expect good service, you get more.

Ask with expectation—"*How* will you rectify this?" instead of
"Can you?" Don't ask if they'll help. The choice is from where and
how help will come. At a conference, Heather said her hotel had no
hot water for three nights. She complained to no avail and felt she
should pay less. I advised inquiring about how much she'd get, not
if. She says:

> I went downstairs, bracing for a rumble, and said, as you practiced
> with me: "I'd like to know what adjustment the hotel will make to
> my bill because of the. . . ." Before I'd even finished, the manager
> made an offer Um . . . OK! So no rumble necessary, and I wound up
> paying $55 a night for Manhattan.

When you talk to someone in customer service:

▶ *Keep a paper trail of communication.* Immediately write down the date, time, and rep's name. Note the highlights of the conversation. If you call again, continue on that page with date and name as backup for going higher.

▶ *If the person can't resolve it to your satisfaction, insist on speaking with a supervisor or person in charge.* Don't explain over and over. I no longer argue. I just insist on getting someone else.

▶ *Give them reason to value your business.* Explain how long you've been a customer or that you're new and their good reputation attracted you. "I'd hate to have to ruin it." (Smile.)

▶ *If all else fails, go higher.* Go to the top. For corporations, write to the CEO. Call to get a name. Use the resource directory at http://consumeraction.gov for corporate office info. The Public Service Commission is terrific for assisting with problems relating to a utility or cable service. After going through hell with my cell phone company, I wrote a businesslike letter to the president. I'd kept a written record and included a summary with names and details. A credit and apology arrived quickly.

Many women keep quiet in restaurants and take what's given to avoid causing trouble. They'll eat undercooked steak, apple pie after ordering cherry, or food they don't like. In my DoorMat days, I'd *never* complain. Friends encouraged me to get what I wanted, but it was too painful. If someone stood up for me, I cringed and apologized but learned that speaking up puts me in charge of my life. Zina agrees:

A friend complained that the menu indicated her fish was healthy, but it was greasy. I suggested sending it back and got "I'll eat it. It's not so bad." As she looked at her plate with dismay, I said she should enjoy food she pays for and explained the problem to the waiter. He immediately said he'd be happy to bring something else. She thanked me profusely while enjoying her meal.

I once ordered a full dinner, planning to take half home. I asked for a doggie bag, but the waiter goofed. It got thrown out. He apologized and actually expected me to pay for a whole dinner without the other half! I nicely but firmly insisted on getting my food. Could he do it or should I ask the manager? I got a full portion, freshly cooked. Why not speak up? What concerns you?

▶ *The waiter will get mad?* It's his job to serve what you want.
▶ *The waitress won't like you?* You'll be history in an hour.
▶ *The waiter will think you're a problem?* They're used to food being sent back.

Don't apologize for asking. It's your right to enjoy your food. Most waiters graciously accommodate. Why eat something you don't like and pay for it? People Pleasers suffer. I enjoy a good meal!

On the other side, don't forget that people get busy and can't always jump for you. Have patience. A salesperson can't help you if she's helping someone else. A waitress can do only so much at once. Speak up, but also be considerate. Express your needs, but smile and say you understand when they frantically say they're sorry for not being faster. Courtesy gets the best service!

11

Being on Top in Romance

"So live that you can look any man in the
eye and tell him to go to hell."

—JOHN D. ROCKEFELLER JR.

A NEED FOR A man can weaken the strongest resolve and turn you into a DoorMat for a guy who shows zippo appreciation. There are many terrific men. But it's better to keep your distance, and your cool, until one earns your trust, with actions, not just sweet words. People Pleasing gets most intense if you buy the erroneous belief that you need a man to be complete. Were you taught that marriage and kids are more important than developing as an independent woman? Romance portrayed in movies doesn't reflect real life, yet we hope for it! Very successful women whine about feeling like losers for being single.

NOTE TO SELF: When you believe you're incomplete without
a man, you won't be complete with one.

A common complaint is "Why do men treat me poorly? I try so hard." Answer? You let them. Hello! If you make a man the most important factor in your life, you give him power to control it. Instead, maintain your own identity in a relationship and expect to be treated well. If a guy pulls jerky moves, refuse to tolerate them! Men know a Nice Girl on Top will exit if they go too far. Let him know you're one of them. Don't manipulate or play games to get treated well. Just living as an empowered woman sends a message.

✺ Why People Pleasers ✺ Have Less Fun

. . . .

"Love yourself first and everything else falls into line. You really have to love yourself to get anything done in this world."

—Lucille Ball

You can hurt your relationship by accepting traditional roles and keeping quiet about what bothers you. People Pleasers tolerate unacceptable behavior. If you keep giving, while stewing inside, guys take advantage or get turned off. Andy explains:

If a woman gives too much to a man, he'll take her for granted. She comes across as too easy. I can't stand when a woman says what I want to hear instead of what she really thinks. Then I don't know what's sincere or just for my benefit. I don't like her doing things she feels she has to for me, rather than wanting to.

Creating Relationship Trouble

Being a guy's personal DoorMat will *not* keep him. He may take and then run, since dating a DoorMat gets tiring. Besides, do you want someone who stays just for favors? Dave explains:

> *Being too giving becomes a turnoff. If someone constantly sacrifices her own needs, it isn't healthy for her or the relationship and can actually push the person away. Most men don't want to be taken care of or babied. There's a healthy medium as to how much one person should give in a relationship. Finding a wholesome balance between two people is the key. It would likely freak me out if someone constantly catered to me and didn't pay attention to her needs.*

Have you made excuses to stay with someone who often made you unhappy? Do you remember sweet times or concoct a logical reason to accept his baggage? Staying with someone who makes you unhappy keeps you stuck in DoorMatville. Women delude themselves with reasons to hang in:

- ▶ "I'm getting older and must take what's available."
- ▶ "There are much worse, so I'd better keep him."
- ▶ "He's OK some of the time, and I'm not perfect either."
- ▶ "It's wonderful when he treats me right, so I tolerate the bad."
- ▶ "I have no choice. That's how men are."

You do have choices! Women aren't responsible for making relationships work. Do you apologize if *he* hurts you? Many women do. But a healthy relationship is two people working together. Being convinced it's your fault that he broke his promise or hit you is manipulation. People Pleasers take responsibility—Nice Girls on Top refuse to! You can't fix a bad relationship. Change your response and he may wake up. But trying harder to please never works.

 NOTE TO SELF: A relationship is one-sided if you please him to ensure that he stays.

Do you enter a relationship hoping he'll change into your Prince Charming? Why court disappointment? *You* can change only *you*. Both sexes learn habits from stereotypes they were exposed to while growing up. Understand them and deal without anger. But deal! In a support group, Wendy said:

> *Brett's a good husband and loves me. But he gets crazy if I don't go straight home from work. If I take a class, he says I'm not being nice. Sometimes he gets nasty and deletes messages when friends call. He assumes a right to expect me home since I'm his wife. I get angry but remember my mother catered to Dad. I hate to defer but don't want Brett angry. He has no right to keep me from friends, but tradition says I should put my husband first. So I always feel guilty.*

Wendy became sneakier. Yet she couldn't totally accept Brett as unfair since she was raised to be nice and put her husband first. After the group she struggled but took small stands. It takes soul-searching and consciousness to accept that you're entitled to break with stereotypes. Don't be angry with men. They're victims too! Many don't like feeling responsible for a woman's security. James explains:

> *Women act like all men want to take charge. I hate pressure to make my girlfriend feel secure. I'm insecure too! I get stress at*

work, and at home Charla needs me to fix something or be her strength for her. Women say they want men who express feelings, but when I try, I'm advised to take it like a man. Women think all pressure is on them, but I didn't choose my role either.

What People Pleasers Need from Men

I've been in the trenches with women who live to please men and equate happiness with having a man. Then I had a revelation! I'd lost sight of being happy. Hello, Daylle! Being happy is not sitting home waiting for his call. It's not tolerating disrespect. It's not being on edge that he'll leave if I express disapproval. It's not focusing on his pleasure in bed, settling for what he gives. Happiness is not letting his needs trump yours. For a healthy relationship, get a life! Dave agrees:

Personally, for me to even go out with someone, she has to have her own life. I'm not sure anyone wants someone to be dependent. It's not attractive.

> **NOTE TO SELF:** Insults, yelling, unfair blame, and other verbal poison is abuse. Many women say mental abuse is worse than physical pain.

When you make yourself happy, you control yourself with men. People Pleasers settle just to have someone. Nice Girls on Top are complete on their own. People Pleasers seek men to fulfill needs that Nice Girls on Top fulfill themselves:

▶ *Being provided for.* You're something of a kept woman if you're there to be taken care of.

▶ *Security and reassurance.* How secure do you feel being dependent on a guy?

▶ *Validation.* You're not a better person for having a man. True reinforcement of your worth comes from *you.*

▶ *Attention.* Do you need to be with him constantly? That means his life is yours.

▶ *Love.* If you don't love yourself, you won't attract healthy love. If your life has holes, having a guy won't fill them!

Men recognize needy women. Some take advantage. Do you make excuses to avoid breaking up and losing your completeness? Step back from romance needs and get a life! Create your own security. Tara says:

> *I bought the dream. My goal was finding the man who'd give me happiness. Without one I felt a lack—of security, love, meaning. But I realized I wasn't happy with one. I had good times and momentary relief. But I always focused on him being happy, tolerated what bothered me, and deluded myself that I felt special. So I took a break. Spent time alone, pursuing what I enjoy. Life without a man became happier than ever. My new boyfriend is attracted to my having a life.*

Making you happy first and giving yourself a life attracts healthier men and a win/win relationship—you win if he makes you happy/you win if he doesn't since you have a life, with or without him.

EXERCISE: List what you think you need from a relationship. Ask yourself what's on that list that you can give to yourself even if you'd rather get it from a guy.

What Nice Girls on Top Need from Men

Nothing!

It's delicious to be with someone who treats you well and loves you for you. *Wanting* a man is much healthier, and more attractive, than *needing* one. Needing gives a guy too much importance. Wanting keeps you selective. Robin says:

> *I had a major disagreement with my guy, who's been spoiled by other women. Before I'd have begged forgiveness so he wouldn't be mad at me. Now I have a life I love and no longer allow him to control my thinking. When Harry tossed me the "my way or the highway" routine, I showed him the door. He was stunned but apologized, and we compromised. He knows he must be considerate or lose me and finds that attractive!*

The quest for a man makes us lose sight of true happiness. My epiphany came when I missed a guy I'd broken up with but realized I'd been more miserable with him. Happiness became my barometer. I've asked clients, "Are you happy?" and gotten "But I love him!" or "He's better than my last guy" or "He doesn't mean to hurt me." Yada! Yada! We often don't consider whether a relationship brings joy. Creating your own life is the foundation. Todd says:

> *I dated a woman who said she couldn't stand being alone. I said I'd call, but she said, "You won't. No other man has called." That made me not want to call. Neediness and desperation are so unattractive! Women need to learn to be OK on their own. I can't give one something she doesn't already have.*

I was blessed to learn to make myself happy. If you *need* a man, prepare to be incomplete. Give yourself what you need to attract a healthy relationship. Jen did:

I'm seeing a guy I like, who said, "I want to make you happy." I laughed and explained this is not his responsibility. Just like to love someone you must first love yourself, I believe to be happy with someone it's important to be happy with yourself on many levels. You can't expect your significant other to turn on a light switch to your overall happiness. It's your responsibility! It is not my boyfriend's to bolster my internal happiness. We can grow and work on our shortcomings together. He can compliment me but can't make me love me! My loving who I am is the core for internal happiness. It took time for me to fully grasp this, but now I know that internal happiness is something that lasts a lot longer than any other happiness I've felt before.

Instead of moaning about what you don't like about him, do more for you! Make yourself happy. Develop a life that revolves around you, not him.

✄ Staying Sweetly on Top ✄
. . . .

"Take your life in your own hands, and what happens? A terrible thing: no one to blame."

—ERICA JONG

IN MY DOORMAT days I let every man milk me dry before we tanked. Now I express needs nicely, once, and change my behavior. If he's disrespectful or abusive—physically or mentally—there are only two choices: suffer or leave. Guess what I'd do!

PREPARE TO TAKE A STAND.

- Alert friends to be ready to keep you busy. Make lots of plans.
- Get involved in organizations or a charity to do things and make new friends.
- Practice going out solo while still with him. Discover the fun of doing everything your way.
- List every way you can think of that he made you unhappy.
- List the benefits of not being in a relationship, like the toilet seat staying down, the fact that you won't have to shave your legs in winter, that life is all about you.
- Save money carefully so you're more solvent to support your own freedom.
- Do something special for *you*. Plan a vacation. Buy tickets to an event you'd love.

Handle Him = Handle You

If you want a happy relationship, forget how friends, the media, and other influences say he should act. Accept him as is—his right to communicate his way and have different behavior and needs. You can change your response to his behavior but not him. *That's reality.* If the original package is unacceptable, find someone else. A relationship is two people. Women aren't in charge of determining the specs of a relationship, though we often treat men like projects, to guide, mold, and fulfill the Prince Charming fantasy. He's entitled to equal input.

Decide which of your guy's habits are unacceptable and which are petty. You have annoying traits too! If his behavior is unacceptable, explain why, nicely. Be prepared to walk. If he believes you'll stay no matter what, he'll continue. Speak with conviction. But, if you want him to ditch his buddies or go somewhere he hates, reconsider. He's entitled to time without you. Why drag him? We sometimes label as wrong almost everything he does that's not our way. Not fair! Lamar says:

> *My wife treats me like some cretin who needs an overhaul. If I don't do it* her *way, I'm wrong. I like to fold jeans into drawers. "They're supposed to be on hangers!" I like slippers by the bed. "They go in the closet." I'm tired after work and need to quietly decompress. "You're supposed to share your day with me." Asking by whose rules invites more grief. I love her but sacrifice my right to be me. She acts like the higher authority. Then she wonders why I'm unaffectionate. I don't feel loving to someone who's always telling me what to do!*

NOTE TO SELF: A good relationship involves compromise about filling needs.

Do you expect chores done your way? While some men do nothing, many would do more—their way. If you want his help, give him a say and be patient. He's not your maid. Criticism won't work. Nor will yelling or complaining. Ask for help nicely and be clear. Men say they'd do more if they got details. "Clean more!" is meaningless. Clarify what you'd like done. Whining "I wish you'd do more" says little. Nicely spell out your needs. Some examples:

▶ "You promised to do laundry, and I'm out of clean socks. I'd appreciate cooperation."

▶ "I was counting on you to pick up Bobby. I had to stop cooking to get him. Can you please try harder in the future or call if you're delayed?"

▶ "I'm sure you didn't mean to, but you left the milk out and it spoiled. Can you please be more careful?"

▶ "You didn't take the garbage cans to the curb as promised. Now they must sit for days. That's unhealthy. How should I remind you?"

Men need specific and logical reasons for your annoyance. Nagging or lecturing reminds them of Mom. Speak to your guy as an adult. Rather than focus on what he doesn't do, explain why doing X and Z would be appreciated. A positive spin works better. Praise his efforts. Involve him in dividing chores. Don't just assign jobs like Mom. If he promised to do one but didn't, explain clearly why it bothers you. Men can be dense! Ask respectfully—not demanding, criticizing, or hinting:

▶ "Take out the garbage!" vs. "I need you to please take the garbage out."
▶ "The garage is disgusting" vs. "I'd appreciate your organizing the garage."
▶ "You're a slob—pick up your clothes!" vs. "I've tripped on your clothes. Can you please put them away?"

Nicely explain that you want a team effort with chores or to resolve a problem. If something is dirty since he didn't do laundry as promised, ask how he can help in a timely manner. If he hasn't painted the garage after months of empty promises, get a list of painters and sweetly ask which to hire. That might get him off the couch. Meghan complained that the women served and cleaned up while the guys relaxed at family dinners. I suggested new rules. Meghan called, excited:

I suggested to the women in advance that we direct the guys to clean up. Some were nervous but agreed to try. During dinner, I announced our plan. The guys snickered, but I explained that either they helped or no more dinners. My sister stayed in the kitchen

to direct. The rest of us girls relaxed. Mom was amazed watching
Dad carry dirty plates. He never helps at home, but he told Mom
she doesn't ask. Judy gave them containers for leftovers, and they
even loaded the dishwasher. All it took was nicely informing them
they needed to help.

When your guy tries, show appreciation even if you want more.
If he doesn't do it as you would, don't do it yourself or criticize.
Thank him for trying and gently guide him. Men respond better
to friendly suggestions than to annoyance. Long-term cooperation
beats a nasty, unproductive confrontation that won't get dishes
washed.

Keeping the Serve in Romantic Ping-Pong

Focusing on you instead of doting on him creates healthier relationships. Let him compete with your life instead of making his
life yours—always—even in marriage. Schedule time with him
instead of always being available. When you have a life, it's your
choice to stay or leave. Don't give a guy sole power over your happiness. When you have a life, he knows you can live without him
and may be busy if he calls at the last minute. Needing him makes
him secure that you'll tolerate his shenanigans. When you're too
busy to revolve around him, he knows he can't get away with stuff.
Yassmin tells herself if a man wants her he'll do what pleases her,
adding "Love is giving and receiving. I do self-therapy to control
my emotions and don't allow myself to get obsessed about him.
That's dangerous!"

NOTE TO SELF: Guys are attracted to independent women.
Some may be intimidated, so wait for the one who isn't!

Women play what I call romantic ping-pong. He serves bad behavior; you pull back. He plays your way—for the moment—and you succumb to his goodies. He's secure again and again serves bad behavior. You pull back, and the volley continues. *Never* go forward completely. Keep your life a priority. Even if he swears to change, keep the serve by continuing to make plans with friends and making your life as important as being with him. Let him worry. This is no game. It's healthy. Let him veg on the couch. Make your own plans. Don't do everything together. Knowing you have a life makes him think twice before playing jerk games. Mala learned:

> *For years, I'd known my marriage wasn't working but, like many women, wanted to do the "right" thing for my children and stayed. Periodically we'd have huge fights. I'd say I wanted a divorce when I'd lost my temper. He assumed I didn't mean it. It always ended with him convincing me to give it more time to see if things got better. After five years of the same pattern, I was completely miserable. One day a shift occurred in my thinking. I realized he would never agree with me about our marriage being over. From his perspective things were fine. I decided it was up to me to take responsibility for my own happiness, regardless of whether he agreed. Saying I wanted a divorce was one of the toughest things I ever did. He responded as always, only this time I didn't back down. When he asked for more time, I said "No! I've tried long enough. There's no more left in me. It's over. I don't love you anymore." Even saying those words now seems cold. But I made a commitment to myself and couldn't back down. He tried all his old tricks, sad eyes, pleading, yelling, crying—even saying I was killing him. I talked to myself the whole time—"Stay strong. Don't back down. You can do this. He won't die. This is important; it's for you." He finally took me seriously. Unfortunately, it was too little, too late.*

Empty threats don't work. If you want more and he won't budge, be ready to leave—no more warnings and chances. If he knows you're serious, he'll try harder. If he doesn't, you're better off solo. John warns: "If you let a man get away with disrespectful behavior, he'll continue, despite your complaints. You must do something to show you're serious." Consistent autonomy keeps the serve in your court—he's competing with your life instead of being it. Love yourself more! Michelle learned:

I'd heard it is impossible to love someone else unless you truly love yourself. Once the full weight of that message set in (finally), I began to articulate my feelings, opinions, and needs a lot better to my partner. I learned to let him in and really be myself. It became apparent that my partner and I weren't suited to each other, but I've now found someone whom I love very much and who loves me the way I deserve to be loved.

Make yourself important, but make him feel important too. Thank him when he cooperates. If he didn't clean the garage, explain that you love him but aren't happy he broke his promise. If you get angry, focus on the situation, not him personally. Calmly explain *why* it bothers you and ask how you can work together for a resolution. Don't react the same way to everything. Rank what bothers you as (a) silly/annoying, (b) he should know better/annoying, and (c) unacceptable. Let your response reflect its level. If you berate him for all of these in the same way, he'll take no complaints seriously. Not recapping toothpaste or being late once is *a*. Being late often is *b*. Being late for an important event or always keeping you waiting is *c*. If you react the same to them all, he'll lump your complaints as nagging and ignore them. Save the very firm for *c* incidents.

If he's hurtful, ask why he does it. If he won't stop, it's your *choice* to accept it. Does your guy have a bad temper? Are you always on edge about setting him off? Does he blame it on you? Unacceptable! He needs counseling, but men often refuse to go. Handle yourself. If he continues, leave and bask in the glow of the empowerment that valuing yourself enough to do it brings!

12

Nice Girls on Top at Work

―――――

"Whatever women do they must do twice as well as men to be thought half as good. Luckily, this is not difficult."

—CHARLOTTE WHITTON

THERE ARE STILL double standards and different expectations for some women in the workplace. *That's reality.* We've come a long way, but progress doesn't make inequities that still exist more acceptable. You can moan to friends or nicely stand up for yourself!

✒ Breaking Old Habits ✒

. . . .

"Nothing gives one person so much advantage over another as to remain always cool and unruffled under all circumstances."

—THOMAS JEFFERSON

TAKING A STAND can be toughest at work when you need the job. More diplomacy is needed. You can feel helpless if you don't feel valued, make less money than men doing the same job, and/or feel deserving of a raise you're afraid to ask for. Replacing old habits with more effective behavior can change that.

Checking Emotions

I can't emphasize this enough, girlfriend! Do whatever you can to keep emotions in check in work-related situations. When I started Revenge Records, I got no respect. But instead of getting angry, I learned to handle myself nicely. If men explode when they lose their tempers, that's considered being a guy. We don't get to do that. *That's reality.* Men don't get asked it they have PMS if they speak up in firm ways. We do. Emotional outbursts are considered weakness in women. Don't give the boys what they want—reasons not to take you seriously. Stay cool under pressure. Emotions are interpreted:

- ▶ You can't handle responsibility.
- ▶ You succumb to pressure.
- ▶ You let frustration get to you.
- ▶ You're overly sensitive.

Even if that's not true! Forget special assignments or promotions if you're seen as someone who doesn't handle situations calmly. Learn self-control. No matter how much someone pushes your buttons, force yourself to keep a lid on emotions. My mentor told me to bite my tongue, mouth, etc., if necessary to maintain a cool front. Do whatever it takes to sound calm. Afterward, rant privately in the ladies' room, but exit with a calm smile.

NOTE TO SELF:

- ➤ Don't complain to co-workers. They may bite you back.
- ➤ Don't call a friend to rant from work. Someone may hear you.
- ➤ Don't e-mail friends to rant. Companies *do* check. E-mails can be retrieved after they are deleted.

No More Smoke Signals!

If you want to get ahead professionally, practice asking for what you want in a straightforward way. When a guy thinks he deserves a raise, he asks. Women circumvent, complain, or wait for an offer and hesitate to be direct. Many women earn less than men at the same job. Getting angry won't help. Make an action plan to get what you deserve. Don't dance around it. "I don't make enough money for what I do" can be "I expect more." Short, sweet, to the point. It's hard to ask for a raise or promotion if you're taught to take what you get. Get over it if you want to complain less and have more money/power! Prepare first.

▶ Research average salaries for your position. Ask folks at other firms for the pay range. Check payscale.com and salary.com. Read job ads.

▶ List why you deserve a raise or promotion—all your good assets, skills, and what you've done for the company.

▶ Pitch based on why you've earned it, not why you need more money. Prepare points that illustrate your value to the company, like extra skills, computer expertise, running meetings, or editing everyone's reports.

▶ Memorize and practice your pitch. Get help from friends outside the company. Focus on that list to stimulate confidence in your presentation.

▶ Convince yourself first. Use your written ammo to accept that you deserve what you're asking for. Erase apologies or hesitation from your voice.

▶ Have a positive attitude, no complaints. Smile, thank your boss for her time, and mention why you like working there.

▶ Find something nice to say first. As I said earlier, compliments get mileage.

▶ Keep the pitch short and direct.

Never ask in writing! Arrange a short meeting with the appropriate person. Don't pressure her to meet with you. Be patient. Explain that you'd like to discuss your value to the company. It gives the person time to think about it. Ask for more than you want initially to allow room for negotiating. Mara says:

> *I asked for a raise this year. It was hard. I know I'm really great at what I do and that I help bring in a lot of money. But I also really love my job, and I don't want to lose it. I told myself that I deserve it and I'd get it no matter what.*

If what you're offered seems too little, negotiate. Men do. If you know you do a good job, you're entitled to a raise, promotion, or whatever you've earned. Don't minimize your accomplishments. Men are much quicker to take credit for their successes—and yours if you let them! Don't brag, but observe how others express their worth and follow suit. If you're offered less, don't get an attitude or get upset. Have a response to open negotiations, softly, with a smile:

▶ Don't discuss what male colleagues earn. Explain, "I've researched, and $40,000 to $60,000 is the range for what I do. I get only $35,000." Let him talk next.
▶ "I was expecting more. I believe I deserve at least $____. I'd appreciate your reconsidering the offer."
▶ If you negotiate a fee for a specific project, ask, "Is that the best you can do?"
▶ If you do tasks that aren't in your job and fill in for people at a higher level, ask for a promotion that includes what you've been doing, with a better job title.

NOTE TO SELF: Negotiating is expected of men. You earn respect by asserting your right to be paid your worth.

Don't get intimidated if your boss plays hardball. Hanging in may throw him. Some people try to intimidate women. Tough it out! Take the playing field and set the tone. Even if you're terrified, force a facade of cool confidence. The more you seem anxious, the more power you give up. The less desire shown, the more likely they'll acquiesce. *You* must accept your worth first!

"I'm Not Taken Seriously Because I'm ____"

Being pretty, being petite, and looking young are all excuses for not succeeding! Don't play victim! While you may have to work harder to prove yourself, you can! Older men may associate you with their daughters and talk that way. They can relate to a young guy being a go-getter through their own memories. No matter what, people take you as seriously as you take yourself.

Avoid being cutesy. It encourages inappropriate behavior. When I began my record label, men teased, flirted, and humored me, not expecting me to get far. I hated it, but instead of getting angry, I accepted that they didn't know better. I didn't get angry or defensive or have an emotional reaction, which the men were used to from women they picked on. I taught them that they were wrong to misjudge me by doing well. At first, being underestimated was an advantage. They expected little and were unprepared for my moves. Many small labels didn't get paid, but I always did! I expected to, and I made that clear in a businesslike manner.

When making decisions, be clear and state your recommendations with total conviction. No "I think" type of statements that allude to doubt! Be definite and prepared to back it up. "We must ____. It will improve productivity. Here's why: ____." Wavering on decisions comes across as weak, and people lose confidence. People respect you more when you speak with authority. If someone challenges you, act open to input. Listen, assess what's said, and say that you'll consider it—calmly, with a smile, instead of getting defensive.

No matter your age or size, have a professional demeanor. Studies show that people take women who dress provocatively less seriously. While you should be true to yourself, like it or not, even women don't take women in short skirts, low-cut shirts, or tight clothing seriously. Studies found women in managerial positions who dressed in sexy attire were viewed as less intelligent. It looks like attracting guys is your main goal. Don't sabotage yourself by doing this. Estelle says:

> *Although our office has a business-casual policy, I make it a rule to dress professionally every day. As a petite woman, I do not believe that I would be taken seriously at all if I came to the office looking "cute." I would rather dress the part, be a nonconformist, and feel like a professional.*

Wear whatever increases your confidence. When you take yourself seriously and let it show, other factors don't matter. One of my music industry mentors looked much younger than her thirty-five years and was small. But once she spoke, men knew the deal. She did a great job, carried herself professionally, and didn't accept less than total respect. Make sure your demeanor demands respect even if you're a little insecure, using the tips in Chapter 4.

✍ It's Called Being Professional ✍

. . . .

> *"Confidence is the inner voice that says you are becoming what you are capable of being."*
>
> —ANONYMOUS

YOUR REPUTATION IS important in business. First impressions stick and can precede you. Be careful to set the right tone for respect and avoid being the target of negative talk. Treating people with respect and sincerity creates good working relationships.

Speaking Up

People Pleasers don't interrupt at meetings or stop others from interrupting them to avoid seeming rude! When you're passive, it's hard to get attention. Men speak up, so why not you? Sounding sure of yourself gives you more validity, and you get listened to more carefully.

> **EXERCISE:** List everything you'd like to say at meetings that you've been too nervous to try. Practice making points with authority so people know you're serious about your position when you speak up.

Many people say they're scared to speak in front of a group. But it gets you noticed. Remember how in school teachers favored those who raised their hands? Nice Girls on Top look for every opportunity to present opinions and ideas. Speaking up at a meeting, especially early, shows you're a go-getter. Even if it's scary, you can conquer fear of participating in work discussions. During a meeting or brainstorming session, interrupting each other is common. Women who show initiative level the playing field, especially when men dominate the discussions.

▶ Consider what's the worst that could happen if you joined the discussion? Do people get fired or humiliated if they're not perfect?

▶ Study how men communicate and jump into discussions.

▶ Arrive early to relax and do some deep breathing.

▶ Be very prepared with suggestions. Check your notes before speaking.

▶ Try the one point you're most confident in first.

▶ Watch for an opening, take a quick deep breath, and jump in.

▶ Don't excuse yourself for interrupting unless everyone does.

▶ Get your point across in as few words as possible, with conviction.

▶ Be conscious of your tone and pace.

▶ Look around the table as you speak to address the whole room.

To make an important point, begin to speak, pause, and look around the room before continuing. It commands attention and shows confidence. People may interrupt to intimidate or test you. Holding your ground earns you respect. If someone interrupts when you want to continue:

▶ Immediately say "I'm not done yet."

▶ If possible, continue speaking.

▶ Lift your hand as a signal to wait for you to finish.

You don't need to be confrontational to hold your own at a meeting. Own your right to participate. Interrupting gets you heard. It's OK for men, and you too!

Good Work Habits

How you respond to situations or handle responsibilities impacts the impression people get of your value to the company. If you're asked to do something and aren't sure what to do, don't give up or try unsuccessfully. Ask questions. Is there someone you can work with? Complaining about how hard it is won't make a positive impression. Learn more! Estelle says:

Although it's easy to remind colleagues of your accomplishments, the best way to get their attention is to make yourself indispensable in all that you do or at least create the perception that you are. I do this in part by creating an expertise in niche areas of the law and by compiling a wide variety of forms for every kind of task. These activities have created a perception that I am the go-to person for drafting and addressing a variety of legal issues.

NOTE TO SELF: Say yes to requests; then figure out what to do.

Don't blame mistakes on others. Take responsibility for your actions and apologize if you were wrong. People prefer working with those who take responsibility. Playing the blame game causes resentment. No matter how much you don't want someone to know you goofed, don't lie. Admit mistakes confidently, with a smile, and reassuringly explain you've got it under control. Don't make it a big deal. Move on like you're taking charge. You'll earn a lot more respect by being honest instead of making excuses. Jen says:

I have a high-stress sales job that taught me about personal responsibility. To be successful, I have to consistently work hard, maintain a positive attitude, and be accountable for my sales quota. To do this, I develop my skills. The fewer excuses I make, the more I focus on how to get the sale. If I'm thinking of why something didn't happen, then I'm not thinking about how I can make it happen. My mind isn't focused on achieving goals.

Being taken seriously is earned. You may have to pay more dues than men. Don't waste energy griping. Work harder and give yourself a foundation of accomplishment to stand on. Have good work habits. Yassmin says, "I get taken more seriously by trying the best I can." Consciously make a good impression:

▶ Don't do a lot of personal business. It can overshadow the good you do.
▶ Be punctual and meet deadlines. If you promise something, deliver on time. If you run late, notify the person. Be prompt for meetings, stay on schedule, return calls quickly, work late when needed, and arrive on time to make an awesome impression.
▶ Watch your language. Cursing makes a bad impression.
▶ Don't act competitive. It creates enemies.
▶ Periodically clean your work space. Looking at big stacks makes you feel out of control. Organizing enhances confidence and looks better to others.

✨ Negotiating Office Politics ✨

....

"Believe in yourself and there will come a day when others will have no choice but to believe with you."

—CYNTHIA KERSEY

BE CAREFUL ABOUT getting involved in office politics. Talking about others breaks rungs on the ladder to success. Do your best to create a positive work environment, even among negative people. Don't get caught up in gossip or putting colleagues down. You can maintain peace in a war zone with soft words and a big stick to go with them.

Good Work Attitude

A good attitude works better than complaining. A team player is valued and a cheerful attitude appreciated. People seek those on their level. When you begin to achieve more and make strides, some folks may get uncomfortable or envious. Your success can remind them of what they can't achieve. It's unfair but normal. Annoying things happen. Handle them with grace and a smile to make a better impression and feel more peaceful. Sometimes you do need to take a stand that won't be well received. Mara advises choosing your battles:

Choose the ones you're willing to go to bat for. At my last job, I took a three-week vacation. When I got back, they had redistributed all my accounts among the other workers and decided I would take one for the team and do all the new accounts. I refused and walked out. They closed one month later.

 NOTE TO SELF: Save gripes for friends.

If someone annoys you, excuse yourself and calm down. Consider whether responding is necessary. If the behavior is consistent, avoid that person. Beila got upset when a co-worker spread negative rumors about her. She was questioned about it. Beila's first instinct was to rant to her boss but instead says:

I explained to my boss, nicely, that the rumors were unfounded. He said he had no reason to believe them. I avoided those who might spread rumors, developed better relationships with more positive people, and focused on doing the best job I could. The rumors died fast. My boss eventually transferred the person suspected of starting trouble.

Do you work with someone who always sours your mood with her persistent problems? Try to avoid those types. When there's no choice, avoid eye contact or even face contact to keep it less personal. No matter how tempting, don't have personal discussions or give advice that immerses you in their issues. Be friendly but aloof. Change the subject to something work related. If she asks why you don't listen to her whine, nicely explain that your time is limited and you like to talk business—personal stuff makes you uncomfortable. If he asks you to have a drink after work, say your free time is tight and you need to scoot out—unless it's someone you truly want to get to know better. But if it will stir up gossip, reconsider.

Keeping peace is better than working amid anger. If someone bothers you, try speaking one-on-one, nicely. Put yourself in her shoes. Understanding her motives can take the sting out of words. Judy told us in a class:

> *When I started my present job, Toni, my supervisor, took me under her wing. She made suggestions about my appearance, which I ignored but thanked her for. Toni wanted me to emulate her, but I preferred my way. After my promotion, she got cooler but continued offering advice. As I advanced, Toni became more critical and then warned that if I didn't stop being a bitch I'd lose my job. It was such a slap in the face. I almost quit.*

Judy succeeded without help. Toni was used to gratitude for her guidance and resented Judy's not wanting it. Toni probably interpreted Judy's independence as an insult to her experience. If a colleague questions your approach to a task, don't argue or get defensive. Calmly explain that while you appreciate her, you prefer your way, and explain why. Judy shared the ending:

I tried being more sensitive and asked Toni's advice occasionally to show respect. I explained to her over a relaxing lunch that while I had a lot of admiration for the job she did, I worked best in my own way. We still don't love each other but work together without name-calling.

Find diplomatic ways to handle people who anger you. Judy was glad to have peace at work using compassion and kind gestures. For a serious problem, ask your supervisor for advice. Don't criticize the co-worker. Just explain the difficulty and ask for suggestions to handle it. Of course this is a roundabout way of complaining! But it looks better and makes the supervisor part of the resolution.

Let colleagues know you value them. Treat them with respect even when they don't seem to respect you. Carly was furious when Chris, on her support team, sent inappropriate paperwork to a client without running it by her first. It was a serious breech that could have cost her the client. Carly's instinct for an angry confrontation kicked in, but she calmed herself:

An angry confrontation always creates bad feelings. Being in charge, I wanted to set a tone of working together well, not my way only. Calming down first restored control. I called Chris in and forced a smile, asking why she'd sent the paperwork since I said I wanted it done differently. She explained this was how it had been done before. I explained why it could damage my relationship with the client. She apologized for not getting my approval. I drafted a document making the procedures clear. Everyone is working together, with no hard feelings. I feel more respect.

Handling Colleagues

It's fine to be friendly, but draw the line at wanting everyone to like you. Otherwise you may try too hard to please, making it hard to enforce rules. Someone may act like your friend, but be careful, at least until she's truly earned your trust over time. Things get repeated and exaggerated. No matter how friendly someone is, share little. If she asks how you are, you're great. Don't share personal problems. Estelle says:

> *I have found a way to stay in the loop without resorting to engaging in it. I have always been more comfortable around support staff and nonlawyers in all my jobs. These friendships have allowed me to transcend office politics as I am just as likely to find out who is getting what in terms of money and assignments through the secretaries and about firm developments, new hires, etc., through Reception. The gatekeepers are the antidote to politics.*

NOTE TO SELF: Nicely avoid your co-workers' personal business.

Avoid gossip and negative office talk. It's unprofessional and can return to bite you. If you're accused of being a snob for not chatting about personal details, explain you're uncomfortable with it. Some folks just can't shut up. A co-worker may often barge into your office to gossip. Do you stop work and politely listen? Use body signals to deflect her. Keep working. Look at your watch a lot. If you consistently don't listen, she may find more receptive ears. If it continues:

▶ While in transit, slowly walk away, saying "I'll let you get back to your work." Then walk faster.
▶ If a yakker approaches your desk, grab the phone, keep working, and nod to indicate you're tied up. Thank her for understanding before she replies.

▶ Explain how busy you are and, smiling, add you're sure he understands since he must be busy too.

Handle petty problems with diplomacy. If Jim takes your pens, ask, with a smile, when he can replace them since you need them. If slow Kim pushes her work on you, while making personal calls and sending personal e-mails, nicely explain that you have your own work. If Anna thinks it's OK to go through your desk, say you'd appreciate her asking first. Thank her for understanding before she can argue! If John in the next cubicle is loud, explain that he may not realize his voice carries. If he continues, nicely but firmly say you need him to lower his voice. If he refuses, ask a senior person if you can move or if she can advise you how to handle Mr. Big Mouth. Once again, it's important to choose your battles. Let small things slide.

If a co-worker subtly picks on you with sarcasm, just smile, or even laugh to defuse it. Ignore her when possible. And be nice if possible. Don't address problems with others present. If someone creates static, discuss it privately. If that doesn't work, use my technique to seek advice from someone higher instead of complaining. Ask for suggestions about handling the situation. It gets the message across and sounds more professional. Samantha says:

Robert and I have equal status, yet he'd switch client files the boss divided between us, keeping the better ones. Robert laughed when I questioned it. Not wanting to be a complainer, I got the boss right after he complimented my work and asked if he could give me new files directly. I laughingly said somehow my good clients always ended up in Robert's stack. Ha-ha. The boss understood, and now I get them directly. Robert called me a bitch for complaining. I calmly said I didn't complain and asked what he'd call someone who stole my clients, all with a smile. Now he knows he can't pull nonsense on me!

> **EXERCISE:** If someone continually picks on you or has inappropriate behavior, log it in a notebook. For each incident, write the date, time, and specific behavior, one under the other. If she goes too far or causes trouble, you have details to show.

Has someone talked behind your back? Confront her nicely. Explain what you heard and say you'd prefer to ask her than listen to gossip. In the future, if she has a problem, ask her to please address you instead of the grapevine. She'll probably expect nastiness. Catch her off guard by nicely asking her to work with you to avoid misunderstandings. Smile and thank her for listening. Women who talk behind your back don't expect women to be direct. Always speak in person.

If you're in a position of responsibility, find the line between being friendly and enforcing rules. If someone slacks off, speak with concern. Ask what's wrong. If she arrives late, say nicely but firmly, "I need you on time. Is that a problem?" If it is, explain that her job requires her to be in at 9:00 A.M. What can be done? Sometimes leaving the job is the option for someone with outside problems that affect work. Ask if she can work with you. If she can't, you may have no choice.

Being known as someone who's friendly, courteous, professional, and above the gossip train earns the most respect. When you do a good job too, you're seen as a valuable employee. It creates better work relationships in the long run and can lead to promotions!

Getting Along with the Boys

If you work in an all-boys domain, use more diplomacy. They may seem like a formidable group, but most are fine individually. Leave your attitude home and accept that men have their own ways of doing things. Female audio engineers have complained to me about how tough it is being the only woman in the studio. Men weren't welcoming. That makes sense, since we often enter their domain trying to change it. The women admitted getting upset with the less than pristine bathroom facilities, which the men were fine with. They also objected to frequent cussing. If men are used to one way and you arrive trying to change it, why should they be happy you're there?

There are two important things to understand about men, whether at work or at play, that can elicit more cooperation. One, if you want guys to take your needs more seriously, be specific about why you need it. Ranting about what you don't like will get ignored or ridiculed. Men have different needs. If what you complain about wouldn't bother him, he may pooh-pooh it. Give him clarity! For example, you may be upset after a man yelled that your body excited him or he'd love to get into your pants. Meanwhile, Bob is thinking he'd love a woman to say that to him. What's the big deal? Explain *why* it bothers you and how it makes you feel. If you want him to take down his sexy calendar, irately saying it offends you will get scoffed at. Nicely explain the specific reasons it offends you. Men need to understand before they can empathize or agree.

Two, while it's always best to talk one-on-one, it's even more advantageous with guys. Together they get that male brotherhood mentality of making fun and acting macho. They also need to "look good" or show off in front of each other. Individually, each can be a pussycat who listens respectfully and wants to help you. If you feel a "them versus you" attitude, invite one to coffee or ask to speak alone. Explain you know things aren't good between you and the guys but you'd like to get along better. Ask for his advice for achieving that. If you sound reasonable and kind, he may soften and become an ally. Once he's friendly with you, they may follow his lead. Try talking to each individually over time. As you get to know each other, things can improve—if you lighten up. Whitney says:

> *I was the only woman on my sales team. I expected to feel like an outcast and did. The guys would stop talking when I joined them and spoke differently to me. I developed an attitude. You suggested getting to know them individually. I assumed they wouldn't want to know me. But one at a time, I stuffed my attitude, put on a smile, and found ways to speak to each alone. After several lunches and coffee breaks, they got to know me as a person, not the only woman. I also used my sense of humor more to break the ice. It's really improved our interactions. Now we really are a team!*

Choose battles carefully! And learn to be a good sport. Roll with their ways as much as you can, and slowly implement changes that are most important to you, with humor and a flexible attitude. Don't demand change. Bring some cleaning stuff and tidy the bathroom. Nicely explain why you're uncomfortable if it's not clean. With a smile, ask if they'd be a bit more careful in there instead of indignantly saying they keep it filthy. The female engineers came to me with a confrontational attitude. I advised chilling their jets. Guys aren't enemies. They just need to slowly acclimate to a different environment. Bring in feminine touches gently. I've always gotten along with men because I respect their right to be different and don't try to force my ways on them. A box of doughnuts helps too!

EXERCISE: Observe how men handle situations differently from you. Decide what you can learn from, whether using some of their techniques or seeing what's ineffective.

Handling Your Boss

Women in my workshops often complain about an unresponsive, overly demanding, or disrespectful boss. If you need your job, you can feel helpless to stand up to him or her. But you can—nicely! I believe most people in high authority are decent souls under pressure. When you approach a boss with that belief, communication can be easier. Acknowledging how hard he works and the stress he's under can soften him to hear you out more objectively. Remember, the boss is a person. Think in terms of having a discussion instead of a confrontation. Rhonda felt very disrespected by her boss. We made a plan. She says:

> *Herb had no manners and ordered me around, demeaning me for little things, with no appreciation for what I did well. I asked for a meeting and was prepared with specifics for why I deserved respect and appreciation. I opened by saying I liked my job and softly asked if he thought I did anything right. He was shocked. I was the best assistant he'd had! I kindly explained he only criticized. I acknowledged he's under pressure and may not mean to be disrespectful, but his criticism and lack of kind words hurt. He apologized! I asked for more sensitivity. He agreed. When he forgets, I smile and remind him.*

A common complaint is that the boss expects too much and overloads work. If you're told you must work several Saturdays and don't get overtime, ask for extra time off when work slows down. If you're given another project or client and your workload is overflowing, don't complain. Instead, thank her for her belief in you and ask her to go over what's on your plate to give you guidance about how to tackle it all, since you don't want to give less than your best to everything. It can help her see how much you have.

If it doesn't seem doable, ask for advice on prioritizing the work or who can assist. Be prepared with a list of what you have to do and estimations of how long it takes to do each, without complaining. Asking for advice sends the message without your seeming whiny. Explain to your boss you'd like to do as good a job as possible but it's harder if you rush through so much. If you often get extra duties, discuss your job description or ask for a promotion/ raise to accommodate additional responsibilities.

> **EXERCISE:** List all the ways that you're an asset to your company. Add to it whenever you accomplish something. Keep it handy for a time when you might want to ask for something or stand up for yourself.

If you feel passed over for a promotion, don't complain. List your accomplishments and why you believe you earned it. Ask for a meeting with your boss. Discuss why you feel you should be considered for a better position or more money. Were you promised a raise by a certain time or a promotion after a complex project but it didn't happen? The tendency is to get angry. And complain. Nicely talk to your boss instead. He may be so busy he forgot. It's up to you to remind him, nicely. Request a meeting and begin by asking if he's satisfied with your work. Then proceed as if getting the raise or promotion is a given. Ask when he can put it through, not whether he will.

Sometimes women are asked to do menial chores or personal errands. The more you do it, the more they'll ask. Address it nicely. When asked to do a task that's below your job description—clean up after a meeting, file papers, stop at the drugstore, etc.—use a friendly, casual tone to explain you have important tasks to do and this isn't a good use of your time. Perhaps someone else could go. Your boss may not realize it bothers you. Gently clarify. Sheri did:

> *Hans was a macho type who barked orders. I was the only girl on the immediate team and often told to make coffee. I'm a graphic designer! The guys laughed. I did it grudgingly. Eventually I sat down with Hans and nicely said that just because I'm a woman, it's not my job to make coffee. When I explained why I didn't like doing it, he understood. He's used to women doing it and took it for granted I would, and I did. Now we take turns.*

Let go of anger. If you agreeably and competently take care of chores, why are you angry to be asked again? Often the boss just needs to be alerted that asking you to do them isn't appropriate. Acknowledge that he's busy but your plate is full too. Ask how he'd like you to prioritize your work to fit in errands. Men sometimes assume women do what's needed. When you do, that's reinforced. Enlightenment with a friendly attitude helps your boss find another way to order his cigars or buy her own pantyhose.

There are times when someone in a senior position may try to sabotage your work. Lorraine said that Louise, whom she reported to, showed contempt for her enthusiasm and positive attitude. She explains:

> *No matter what I did, Louise cut me down. I was hurt but kept trying to please her. When I asked for more detailed instructions, she laughed and said, "Figure it out." Later she criticized my not doing what she wanted. I said I'd asked. That invited more jabs. After a Nice Girl on Top class, I looked Louise in the eye and spoke more confidently. When she slacked off, e-mailing and chatting on the phone, I gave knowing looks and put my energy into doing good work. As I ignored her, Louise picked on others.*

If nothing works and you're miserable, see if you can transfer elsewhere in the company or prepare to apply for another job. Quietly polish your résumé and let people know you're looking to feel more in control. You shouldn't stay if it makes you miserable and no efforts can fix it!

13

Staying on Top

―――――

**"I am the master of my fate;
I am the captain of my soul."**

—WILLIAM ERNEST HENLEY

A s YOU MAKE progress, it's easy to backslide. That's normal. I still consider myself a recovering DoorMat, since insecurity—which happens at times—can tempt me back to being a People Pleaser. It's important to consciously maintain and strengthen your determination and skills for being a nice girl who finishes first. Be more loving to *you* and increase your self-appreciation. The more you feel self-loving, the less inappropriate behavior you'll tolerate.

➷ Making Happiness Your MO ☙

....

"I care not what others think of what I do, but I care very much about what I think of what I do. That is character."

—THEODORE ROOSEVELT

To NURTURE HAPPINESS, sustain a mind-set of being powerful. Set proactive positive goals. For example, "I won't be silent when my colleague takes my supplies" can be "When my colleague takes supplies off my desk, I'll explain that he has to ask." Replace negative thoughts with affirmations that you rock! Revel in each baby step as progress.

Being a Nice Girl on Top Rocks!

Redefine obligations. You owe no more than you can give comfortably, even if people do things for you. It's your *choice*, not your obligation, to help. My stress level lowered when I stopped doing what I didn't want. Being nice for real feels spiritual and peaceful. Being on top empowers your life. Michelle agrees:

> *I feel proud of myself more often, and I don't spend so much time on edge, worrying about what people think of me. Despite what I used to think, this has had a positive effect on how people treat me, and I find that I've earned some more respect.*

Memories of being a People Pleaser keep me resolved when insecurity tempts me to revert. Recall past lousy feelings and let them motivate you to stay strong. Be conscious of how good being a Nice Girl on Top feels! Mara says, "You actually get to be nice and be on top too!" Focus on being the woman you want to be, not to please others. Yassmin moved to New York from a foreign country solo:

> *I've been responsible for myself for eleven years, the time it's taken me to transform and become a better person. The road was really hard. I was sensitive and emotional, always needing that "other" to support me emotionally—anyone was better than no one. My journey to the United States by myself created that need in me. But I learned that happiness is right here with me. No need to look further. Now I'm more confident, independent, and goal oriented. Being a Nice Girl on Top makes me happier every day. I feel*

enlightened, positive, and energetic, not lonely anymore. I smile all the time. The secret is I don't wait to be in a good mood to smile.

Taking control of her life keeps Yassmin smiling! Striving to do your best is a great accomplishment, no matter what the outcome. Be polite and respectful to all. Give to those you want to and turn down those you don't, politely, with a smile. Continue being kind, no matter what others do. Heidi learned:

I think there is always the potential for misunderstanding. We live in a world where no one trusts. Some people get it, and some people don't. But personally, I would never have it any other way. And as long as I'm breathing, I'll come from the light, and as long as I'm living, I'll remain in life's fight.

 EXERCISE: Write down everything empowering you've done recently that you never did before. Use that for strength.

Do you assert yourself with service people and colleagues but turn to mush with family and pureed mush with guys, or vice versa? Building total confidence takes time. Often it grows in one or two areas of your life and not in others. You can bring the confidence from the strongest one into others. I've heard women say:

▶ "I'm tough at work but a wimp with friends."
▶ "I wrap my guy around my finger but am terrified to talk to my boss."
▶ "I'm a confident professional, but my husband and kids walk all over me."

As my career success grew, my confidence increased professionally. But I was still insecure in my personal life, until someone pointed out that I acted powerful in business situations but reverted to little-girl demeanor with family, friends, and guys. Yet I was the same person! She was right. In situations that created insecurity, I began to remind myself that I was the woman who successfully ran a record label and got lots of respect from my male counterparts. It took time, but I slowly incorporated the confident chick into all areas of my life. When I caught myself speaking in a childlike tone with a guy, I silently summoned confident Daylle, reminding myself how powerful I was in my career and that that person was still me. Over time I grew into me all the time.

Consciousness conditioned me to be a confident Nice Girl on Top with everyone. Think about when you feel most in control and slowly integrate that confidence into everything you do. Keep a journal, however informal. It teaches you about yourself, reinforces what works, and serves as a reminder for later of how far you've come, which motivates maintaining your power. Read it back later to revel in your progress and remember what mistakes you don't want repeated!

Be Your Own Cheerleader

Celebrate large and teeny achievements, to embrace the terrific woman you are, increase pride, and reinforce how powerful you are. Don't wait for big stuff. The first time you say no, send yourself flowers. If you ask for something, treat yourself to lunch. If you speak up, toast yourself in the mirror. If you're strong with a disrespectful guy, invite friends to a girls' night out. Make it a habit to recognize achievements and regularly say encouraging words, praise, or "I love you" in the mirror. If I'm down, I say, "You're terrific." I may not believe it then but eventually do! Emily says:

> It began with saying, "You go, girl!" I laughed the first few times, but it grew on me and became my rallying call. When discouraged, those three words push me. It's a double motivation. I like doing

that for me and like that phrase. Saying it in the mirror empha-
sized it more. I use it to build courage or applaud an achievement.
I give other compliments too, but "You go, girl!" is the cheer!

EXERCISE: Do affirmations to acknowledge how terrific you are:
"I rock my world." "I'm smart and capable." "I take care of my
needs first because I love me, and that's good!"

Creating a Two-Way Support Street

Support makes self-empowerment easier. Seek mentors to help
you stay on track. Invite a woman you admire for coffee. Create
a support group of women and meet regularly to encourage each
other. Gather women from work for lunch discussions on getting
ahead. Take care of you, but also give back. Mara says:

As aggressive as I am in getting what I want, I am just as aggres-
sive in encouraging people to get what they want. I am passionate
about people getting their things done. When people tell me that
something isn't working in their life, I'm the first person to try to
help them.

NOTE TO SELF: Stay conscious of how much better your
life is.

What goes around truly comes back. Mentor someone. Help
people when it's possible—not as a draining obligation but as a
choice that sustains you. Winston Churchill said, "We make a living by what we get, but we make a life by what we give." Helping

others makes *you* feel good. Self-sacrificing doesn't. Learn the difference! I help when possible. People are confused that I encourage saying no, yet say yes often. It's for different reasons now. Madison says:

> *My friend Lu does unacceptable things that make friends encourage me to blow her off. I can't count on her, but I know she's unhappy. We've been friends for years, so I show compassion and take care of her apartment when she travels for work, weeks at a time. Nobody understands why. It's a blessing to have someone trusted to mind your home. She has no one else. Doing it is quick, so I'm happy to give her peace of mind.*

Madison knows the joy of giving. Lose any "What do I get out of this?" mentality! Heidi says helping others makes her feel "like I'm doing what I'm supposed to be doing." Trust me; it returns multiplied. But have no expectation of getting back. That creates a blessing. Do volunteer work. Studies show people who volunteer are happiest. Knowing you improve someone's life is a gift to you!

EXERCISE: List what you won't allow people to do anymore. Make a check each time you do something to stop it.

✍ A Few Final Words ✍

. . . .

> *"Our self-image and our habits tend to go together. Change one and you will automatically change the other."*
> —DR. MAXWELL MALTS

I'VE LEARNED MANY lessons on my journey. I've found kinder ways to perceive my body. You may prefer to be thinner. I'd love to be but know the thin fairy doesn't exist, and realistically, I won't lose that much unless I starve or give up all fun eating, which I *won't* do! So I accept my body and use nicer words for it. *Fat* is out. So are *chubby*, *flabby*, and *portly*. I now see my body as womanly— soft and round. Curves are good. So is slender if you think you're too skinny. Words with a positive connotation are more loving and support good self-esteem.

I've learned that the person who can walk away from any situation has the most power. You'll have less to lose by walking away from unhealthy situations *if* you accept that you win when you have a good life and aren't desperate for anything or anyone. Have faith that you'll get what you need in healthy ways. Developing strong faith helped me to be truly on top of my world. When I expect good things to happen, they do. I consciously work with the Law of Attraction to get what I need. Things don't always work out how I'd like. But I know everything ultimately is for a reason and will be OK. And it always is!

EXERCISE: Write down why you enjoy being a Nice Girl on Top.

Do you think, Some people have all the luck, but I don't, and envy others? That affirms good won't come to you. Make your own luck! People say I'm very lucky to have my career, but it's not luck. It's from hard work and determination not to stop until I get what I want. After years of being comatose instead of feeling alive, I won't let anything stop me. Actually, I should say I won't let *me* stop *me*. I was my biggest roadblock to happiness, letting my fears, needs, and lack of confidence guide poor decisions and actions. No more! This Nice Girl on Top is here to stay.

NOTE TO SELF: The great gift you can give yourself is your-self—empowered and happy!

Looking back, I don't regret anything. Life taught me to overcome negatives and appreciate my life now. Many women say it's too late for them. That is so erroneous! You can have a happier life anytime you choose to. People warned me to accept that it was too late to reinvent myself. But it's my only life, and I wasn't going to waste it or give up on creating a happy one. Life is a gift; how you see it is your choice. You can:

▶ View this gift like a lump of coal in your Christmas stocking by feeling unworthy
▶ Limit the pleasure you get from this gift by being scared to use it
▶ Give the gift away by making others more important than you
▶ Unwrap the gift of life slowly and make the most of it

It's all your choice. I highly advise you to make the most of your life. Open the gift. Find new ways to use it. Love yourself enough to take control of people-pleasing habits. As someone who struggled, and hated herself, and took years of baby steps to get out of DoorMatville, I can honestly say that everything—all the work, pain of letting go of bad but comfortable habits, criticism, hurtful responses from others, and losing people—was worth it to be a Nice Girl on Top who's happy and whole! I've learned the blessings that contribute to a satisfying life:

▶ Owning who I am, good qualities and imperfections
▶ Guiding my life according to *my* standards and needs
▶ Feeling self-empowered by taking responsibility for my life

► Embracing a strong spiritual faith that supports every inch of my life
► Taking control over every person and situation by controlling *me*

Now I know how to make myself happy and, in turn, give lots to others. The Law of Attraction is my friend. Back in DoorMatville it was my enemy. Fear of not being liked overwhelmed me. I expected negatives, and they manifested from my thoughts. Now I want and accept goodies, from every direction and in every way. Receiving that sure feels better. Please use my techniques to manifest your own happy life. Take control of your responses to whatever life throws you and you too can manifest what you want. I wish you the blessing of a happy, satisfying life!

Index

❧ About the Author ❧

Daylle Deanna Schwartz, M.S., is a writer, speaker, self-empowerment counselor, and music-industry consultant. She's been quoted in dozens of publications, including the *New York Times* and *Cosmopolitan*, and been on more than three hundred TV and radio shows, including "The Oprah Winfrey Show," "The Howard Stern Show," and "Good Morning America," based on her popular self-empowerment books, including *All Men Are Jerks Until Proven Otherwise*. After being a DoorMat for many years, Daylle empowered herself to take control of her life. She was one of the first women to start an independent record label and learned how to play nicely in the male-dominated music industry while still getting taken seriously. Daylle also writes bestselling music-business books for Billboard Books, including *Start & Run Your Own Record Label*. She speaks for colleges, organizations, and corporations, writes the popular blog "Lessons from a Recovering DoorMat" (www.lessonsfromarecoveringdoormat.com), and is on myLifetime.com's Love Panel. Daylle's website: daylle.com.